# Guiding Principles
# for Life Beyond
# Victim Consciousness

❦

By Lynne Forrest, with Eileen Meagher

# DEDICATION

*To my parents, Jimmie and Estelle, who introduced me to victim consciousness and to the One True Source who showed me the way out.*

# Preface

On the morning of December 16, 2006 I "got" the message. I finally understood that I could no longer coast along, hoping it would work out, praying that I was not getting really sick, but I had to face reality. I was, in fact, increasingly, alarmingly ill.

In October of 2001 I was diagnosed with a serious illness. After consulting with medical doctors and alternative practitioners, I chose to build my immune system using holistic medicine.

But old habits die hard; unhealthy ways of eating and moving through life were so ingrained in my lifestyle that no matter how many times I tried, my flawed efforts could not keep my health from slowly, steadily, declining.

I realized that morning in December that the tools and resources I'd been gathering for years to help others transform their lives were for me; I could see that I had been given many of the tools I needed to restore my physical balance.

My *daily practice* started that very day. That daily time spent in the practical application of principles and techniques for healing and connecting has paid off mightily. Not only have I been led through a process of transformation and alignment that restored my physical health, stabilized my emotions, cleared my thinking and energized my connection with the world around me and with *Source*, I've been given the opportunity to share that process of transformation with others.

Through my *daily practice* of "*aligning* with *Source*," or what I call the *alignment process*, a shedding took place. Physically, I shed more than fifty pounds of extra weight (without dieting). But I shed something even more important than physical weight; I shed layer after layer of unhappy beliefs, of destructive habits, and of defensive reactions that had held me captive my whole life in what I call *victim consciousness.*

Every day, since, I participate in a *daily practice* where I utilize and experiment with the tools I write about in the following pages. I continue to learn so much from that daily sacred time on my mat. I am delighted and eager to pass on what I can of what I have learned. May it be as meaningful and transforming for you as it is for me.

# Acknowledgements

There are so many people to thank. I have wanted to write this book for some time but because of my own full time work as a therapist and other responsibilities, the task seemed overwhelming. I approached a good friend, Eileen Meagher, an excellent writer and a fine editor, for the help I needed to complete this project. She has helped me with the written expression of my ideas and I am deeply grateful to her. There have also been important teachers along the way who pointed me in the right direction at critical junctures, thereby doing their part to make this book possible. They deserve honorable mention.

My first experience with a teaching tool that defined *victim consciousness* was in the seventies. I was studying Transactional Analysis as part of my on-the-job-training for the Hunter Foundation (a health maintenance organization) in Lexington, Kentucky. That's where I was introduced to Dr. Stephen Karpman's "Drama Triangle" (Karpman, S. 1968).

"The Drama Triangle" is a simple and straightforward diagram that explicitly outlines the three primary roles of *victim consciousness (rescuer, persecutor, victim)*. It was the beginning of my work with those who identified themselves as victims, and the origin of my thought about *victim consciousness* (although I did not yet know to call it that) as a separate and identifiable state of consciousness that is treatable, rather than thinking of it as a condition caused by some outside destructive force.

Without that groundbreaking, simple, and straightforward tool – the Drama Triangle – I dare say, I would have nothing to say on the topic of victimization. Since my early introduction to Karpman's Triangle, I've taken the Drama Triangle into the trenches over the last thirty years and used it to help myself, and countless others, to sort through our *victim* patterns. From those hours and hours of research I developed a firm understanding of the consciousness of a victim; I am deeply indebted to Dr. Karpman. His work contributes greatly to what I present here.

There have been a few other important contributors to the ideas I present here. Jacquelyn Small, for instance, is the author of eight or nine books, including <u>Becoming Naturally Therapeutic</u> (1990), and my personal favorite, <u>Transformers</u> (1984). Jacquie first introduced me to the concept of having what she called a "smaller story" and a "bigger story": the "smaller story" (or "lower self") being a limiting definition of ourselves, and the "bigger story" (or "higher self") being the more expanded definition of ourselves.

Through her teaching I began to see the *victim triangle* as an accurate depiction of what it is to live out of our "smaller story" or "lower self." Jacquelyn was also the one who first introduced me to the concept of the "observer self." These concepts play a vital part in the construct I use to describe our two basic life perspectives: *victim consciousness* and *observer consciousness.*

There are two more teachers whose contributions have been critical to the development of ideas presented here, albeit in very different ways.

Byron Katie is the author of <u>*Loving What Is*</u> (2002), <u>*I Need Your Love—Is That True?*</u> (2005) and <u>*A Thousand Names For Joy*</u> (2007). Her work did not come to my attention until more recent years. I had been teaching about limiting *core beliefs* a long time when I stumbled upon her very precise set of tools, called The Work, which consists of four questions and a turnaround. I find these questions extremely easy to use and powerfully helpful in moving us beyond *victim consciousness.* I cannot thank her enough.

And special thanks to the generosity of Katie's husband, Stephen Mitchell, for reviewing Chapter 7 of Part 2 and making valuable suggestions to insure that my adaptation of Katie's process is clear and accurate. I am deeply grateful to both of them.

The other teacher I want to mention is my *qigong* instructor, Jeff Primack, a young man on fire with a mission to share *qigong* with the world for healing and rejuvenation. Jeff exposed me to the concept of *aligning* with *Source* using the physical body as the primary vehicle. I sought out *qigong* as the result of an energetic expression and a release process that I had started to experience spontaneously through my *daily practice.* His teaching showed me how to tap into healing energy through the breath and movement. *Qigong* has greatly accelerated my personal healing and expanded my conscious relationship with *Qi* (Chinese word for universal life energy). Combining the tools of Inquiry that I learned from Byron Katie with the physical forms and techniques of *qigong* (and yoga) has proven to be a powerful elixir for transformation. There are so many more teachers, too numerous to mention to whom I owe a debt of gratitude.

I am grateful to all those who teach me, including those who seek counsel from me. My clients over the years entrusted me with their deeply personal issues and life processes, and, through our walk together, taught me much of lasting value. This book would not be without my clients who dared to face themselves in their burning desire for a better life.

I owe a debt of gratitude to members of my immediate family, namely to my husband, Daniel, who has been my rock of unwavering support. He is my confidante and helpmate. My daughter, Jaquetta Jeffers, has come to be my most trusted assistant. She has worked beside me in this endeavor and believes wholeheartedly in this process. She is not only a strong advocate for this work, but applies the ideas taught here in her own life and serves as a beautiful example to all who know her.

Jaquetta and Zack Czengoldi have been my on-the-ground team for getting this book out. They have been my chief support, my cheering team who gave freely of their time and energy. It was Zack who originally inspired me to write this book. He recognized the hunger of my readers and students for a way out of *victim consciousness* and he "gave me the assignment" to write a step-by-step guidebook to meet that need. Thus began my three year adventure in writing this book.

I also want to acknowledge Nick Lee, my creative stepson and master graphic designer, who created the cover for this book. He took a photograph of our home at Forest Haven and turned it into a cover design that I believe truly transmits the peace and awareness (represented by the interconnecting triangles ) that is possible for us all once we free ourselves from *victim consciousness*.

To these three devoted team members, Jaquetta, Zack, and Nick, I owe huge gratitude for making the physical manifestation of this book possible. Thank you.

My greatest debt of gratitude is to *Source*. My primary relationship with Source is what truly inspired me to share this work; it is through the inspiration I receive from a *daily practice* that I am motivated to write at all. Much of what I say here came to me first in those quiet times with *Source*. Words fail to express the deep, abounding awe and respect that comes in expressing my deepest gratitude for the opportunity to serve *Source* through the ideas presented here.

# How To Use This Book

This is a book about *victim consciousness*. It defines it, and illustrates how it affects our lives. More important, this book provides a way of reframing the way we think about ourselves, our lives, and those around us. It offers an alternative consciousness, a way of observing and exploring life through a filter of guiding principles that allow us to use our life circumstances, no matter what those are, in a way that furthers us, that enlivens us, and that heals us.

I recommend you start at the beginning of this book and read through, simply because the early chapters build a foundation from which the later chapters launch. The book's foundation is based on an energetic understanding of how the mind works; it explains how our thoughts transmit energy; it describes the purpose and function of our beliefs so that we can better understand why and how to transform our thinking. In essence, this book is about learning a process that frees the mind in a way that results in inner calm and peaceful interaction with ourselves and the world.

Start at the beginning and set your intention to have a transformational experience as you read. Participate in the exercises suggested and make a conscious decision to apply what you read here to your current life situation, and then observe the results. Reading in such an active manner will stretch and help develop *observer consciousness*, the antidote to *victim consciousness*.

There are words and phrases that I use repetitively and so have come to have a particular definition/meaning or a specific usage as pertains to the purposes of the process I describe here. These words and phrases are italicized and listed in the glossary at the end of the book for easy reference. Also, the names used in examples and case studies are fictional to protect the confidentiality of those involved.

Share what you learn here with your loved ones by using yourself as a positive example of what is possible. In other words, no matter how much you think they may need to read this material, do not try to pressure them into reading it! Instead demonstrate the difference it is making in your life by the way you interact with them. "Be the change you want to see in them."

# Introduction

I came to this work the way I believe many of us find our paths, by the route of a painfully imperfect childhood. I first learned *victim consciousness* by absorbing it from those around me who were saturated in it and living in it blindly for many years. My desire, first for healing, then for peace, has held me steadfast on the windy, slippery road through family dysfunction, addiction, suicidal depression, divorce, and poverty and onto a road of recovery that has led straight here to sharing what I've learned with you.

There have been many dips and curves but life is like that. Ups and downs, comings and goings, good times and not so good times are the nature of life. I've found that being happy does not depend on outside circumstances, but upon our choice of focus. We must acquire the ability to look somewhere besides the outside world for the love, acceptance and success we seek.

As I mentioned, in my life I have had many hurdles to surmount. Like many of us, I lived an early life deeply steeped in *victim consciousness*; actually I was not familiar with any other kind of consciousness but *victim consciousness*.

My father, a practicing alcoholic, felt persecuted and picked on by the world at large; he certainly had a *victim mentality*. My mother was the classic martyr who sacrificed her own needs for her family. She lapsed periodically into bouts of depression when she felt neglected and unappreciated. My family was saturated in *victim consciousness*; it was virtually all we knew.

My parents were my first teachers. They were my initiators in life. My mother gave me books and esoteric reading on subjects she herself was immersed in: the study of Christ as healer, mystical Christianity, and metaphysics as propounded by teachers from all around the world. By the age of twelve I was reading bits and pieces of Theosophy, Eastern philosophy, and spirituality of all sorts. Reading such literature was an obsession for me back then. Experiencing many of the things I learned about through that reading continues to be what interests me most.

My mother believed in one true God and she modeled a love of exploring our relationship with what she called "Mother/Father God," and what I refer to as *Source*. My mother knew how to make the best out of life situations that were less than ideal, and she died as she had lived, beautifully modeling the grace of acceptance and surrender.

My father played a different role in my life, but one no less important, He saw it as his job to toughen us kids so we could deal with a cruel world (as he saw it); he felt he had to be tough on us. I learned tenacity and determination from him. My dad also introduced me to the world of addiction.

Dad was an alcoholic, by his own definition. Then, in the last fifteen years of his life, he entered the light of a better life through the twelve steps of Alcoholics Anonymous (AA). His role in my life was to introduce me to a lifestyle of addiction (a path I followed into the depths of despair) and then he took me to my first AA meeting and so began my own recovery.

Mom and Dad were two very different types of teachers, equally valuable - though it took me years to see that. (I had to set aside my negative judgments to do so.) I came to see that they represented two distinct teaching styles: my mom modeled by demonstrating positive qualities, characteristics, attitudes, and mannerisms that inspired me and showed me what was possible. My father modeled by contrast. He demonstrated where painful thinking and unhealthy choices lead us. His life served as a painful preview of what could happen if I wasn't careful. He showed me the underbelly of life, introducing me to dark paths of superficiality, confusion, and misery.

I learned tremendously from both styles of modeling. I was challenged by, and deeply blessed by, my parents. I am grateful for my birth family who started me off in life, and, by hook or crook, aimed me in the direction I needed to go to fulfill my present assignment — this book.

As I became more interested in achieving more peace, better health, and positive regard for myself and others, I sought ways to directly apply the concepts I'd spent so much time reading and studying about. My personal life became the place where I did my research; it continues to be my experiential laboratory. I use my daily life situations and encounters to test and verify or dismiss various ideas and approaches in order to expand consciousness.

Through such ongoing research in consciousness I have developed confidence in, and have come to rely upon certain *guiding principles* (see Part I, Chapter 1) about the constructs of reality. Those *guiding principles* are the foundation for the ideas I present here for the purpose of transforming *victim consciousness.*

As mentioned already, I understand *victim consciousness* first hand; I've explored its various faces, its language, and I know something about the beliefs that hold *victim consciousness* in place. This book is my attempt to share what I know about *victim consciousness,* what it is and, more importantly, how to step out of it.

# Contents

## Part II: Transforming Victim Consciousness

# PART I

# A Working Definition of Victim Consciousness

# CHAPTER ONE

# Victim Consciousness:
# A Worldwide Epidemic

The well-known spiritual discourse, <u>A Course In Miracles</u> (Foundation For Inner Peace, 1996), says, "we are never unhappy for the reasons we think." That means that we tend to think our unhappiness comes from some external event or circumstance. But the true reason for our unhappiness is always what we are thinking about an event, never the event itself. To understand that our thinking is the cause of our unhappiness is to initiate the process of freeing ourselves from what I call *victim consciousness*.

*Victim consciousness* is a psychological prison, a mindset so prevalent as not to be recognized as a problem. So many of us don't even question that there might be another way of perceiving life because we automatically assume that our discomfort and misery come from outside causes or circumstances.

We spend much of our time in *victim consciousness*. It is hard for us to see when we are in that state largely because everyone we know seems to perceive the world in the same painful way.

Of course there are degrees of *victim consciousness*. Most of us find ourselves moving in and out of that state of consciousness throughout everyday, regardless of how smart or enlightened we are. If we want to avoid *victim consciousness* and lead more healthy lives, we must begin by shifting the way we perceive ourselves and life in general.

We make that shift by learning to examine our thoughts and beliefs about the things that trouble us. In doing so, we can act to liberate ourselves from *victim consciousness*. Indeed, to move out of *victim consciousness*, we must mentally shift into another, more effective, state of consciousness.

To make the necessary shift out of *victim consciousness* we must learn to see the world in an entirely different way than we, perhaps, are used to seeing it. In essence, moving out of *victim consciousness* requires a reliance on several basic universal principles. Without putting these principles in place, we are bound to go on seeing ourselves at the mercy of a chaotic world which appears to be devoid of *sanity* or purpose.

That shift in consciousness is what this book is about. Through the following pages we embark on a journey that will transform our way of seeing ourselves, others, and the world around us. To start us on our quest for *sanity*, peace, and well-being, I have included here the *guiding principles* that I believe are necessary to successfully shift our mind from *victim consciousness* to its healthier alternative, *observer consciousness*. Belief in these *guiding principles* facilitates our shift from an external focus to an internal one and provides a foundation for understanding that makes escape from *victim consciousness* possible.

The *guiding principles* included here are ones I have gathered from various sources which are too numerous to name. I consider them to be universal, in that most major religions and philosophies, including Christianity, Buddhism, Taoism, as well as many of the more primitive cultures, teach some version of them.

By replacing our old, limiting, and fear-based concepts of reality with such *guiding principles*, we can greatly ease our transition out of *victim consciousness*. It has been my observation that, without a firm understanding of and belief in some beneficent *guiding principles*, we cannot fully come to trust the Universe, or move forward into healing and peace. In other words, if we do not believe in a Universe that is purposeful, meaningful, and benevolent, we cannot rise above *victim consciousness*. We must develop a relationship with a Universal *Source* who we trust can, and does, respond to us, if we are ever to see ourselves as anything more than victims at the mercy of an unkind and unfair world.

# Guiding Principles

1. We are free agents, able to choose what thoughts we believe. The thoughts we believe determine the quality of our life experience.

2. Our thoughts determine our vibrational frequency. When we believe we are at the mercy of a heartless, fearful world, we see ourselves as victims and experience *low-frequency* thoughts and feelings (thoughts that create fear, depression, isolation, resentment, jealousy, etc). When we believe we are protected, loved and prompted by a loving *Source*, we experience *high-frequency* feelings (love, safety, acceptance, joy, satisfaction, peace, etc). The *frequency* we choose to feel (called *alignment*) determines the quality of our life.

3. We are made up of a trinity: mind/spirit, soul/emotion, and physical body. Balancing these three aspects brings us into *alignment* with the highest possible *frequency*: Source.

4. The world acts as a mirror that reflects our own state of consciousness. We project our beliefs onto the world where they are reflected back to us. We then react in ways that prove to us that what we believe is true. We tend to think our beliefs come from our life experiences, but the opposite is true: our experiences most often come from what we believe. Our beliefs create our *personal reality.*

5. Our beliefs become the *personal reality* we see and experience in physical form. In other words, we manifest our beliefs. If we have beliefs that breed feelings of peace and harmony, we will see peace and harmony all around us. If our beliefs are full of strife and conflict, then strife and conflict will be our *personal reality.*

6. Life is cyclic in nature. Like a wheel, life goes round and round; sometimes we are on top of the wheel, sometimes we are on the bottom of it, but how we see these rotations determines how we are affected by them. We either perceive ourselves as victims and feel at the mercy of life's ups and downs, or we move into *observer consciousness* and *witness* life as a reflection of our own mind.

7.  All of our feelings and behavior come from what we think and believe and not from external causes. There are no exceptions. In other words, we act the way we do because of the thoughts we believe. We automatically act according to the beliefs we hold.

8.  What we focus on expands. Attention is a way of directing energy and automatically feeds whatever we are paying attention to. That means the more we resist something the bigger it gets.

9.  Whatever we judge and condemn within ourselves, we deny and then project it onto something or someone outside ourselves. What we judge as unacceptable in others is something we have not admitted or accepted in ourselves.

10. There are no mistakes, no coincidences in life. Everything happens for a reason and/or has a purpose. To see it any other way is to be in *victim consciousness.*

11. There is another *Reality.* It is the deep peace that is always available in the eternal, present moment, no matter what else is going on.

12. We are emanations of what I call the One Universal Mind, hereafter referred to as *Source,* that is ever present and always radiating its benevolent Light (consciousness) upon us.

13. Everything is made of *Source* energy and vibrates at its own particular *frequency.* We are vibrational beings who are attracted to (and who attract to ourselves) people and situations with a similar *vibrational frequency.*

14. *Source* is always here for us. It reaches out to us just as we seek it. It never stops supporting us. It breathes us, and it is closer to us than our own skin.

Having studied these *guiding principles*, we are ready to explore our energetic interaction with the world around us. In the chapters that follow, we will learn in detail about the nature of *victim consciousness*, about the energetic nature of thoughts, about the nature of feelings and beliefs. We will also learn about our *core beliefs* and how they dictate our life expression. We will examine tools, such as <u>Karpman's Drama Triangle</u> *(1968)*, and seek to better understand the nature of our own *core beliefs* and the role they play in our lives. Perhaps most importantly, we will follow a step-by-step guide helping us break the victim cycle and freeing us from *victim consciousness*.

*How Victims See the World*
The nature of the lens through which we tend to perceive life is rarely suspected as the source of our suffering. That limited (and limiting) lens is commonly accepted, by us and others, as a given, as normal. Our pain and suffering then, we also consider to be normal, to be part of the human condition. But this narrow conception of the word "normal" generally means typical or expected. It is not necessarily synonymous with the word "healthy." In fact, far from promoting health, the "normal" state of *victim consciousness* generates misery for ourselves and the world.

For instance, we may think it "normal" for a new mother to experience postpartum depression, in the sense that it is a common occurrence for women who have just given birth to go through some degree of depression. But a "normal" occurrence does not necessarily make it a healthy one. Likewise, *victim consciousness* can be considered "normal" because of its prevalence. But it is far from being a healthy state. Those of us who view life through this narrow lens of what it means to be normal are in *victim consciousness* and thus see ourselves as *victims*. We see ourselves as powerless over or at the mercy of something outside of ourselves and we react accordingly. We blame something or someone external to us for our unhappiness.

*Victim consciousness* generates a "they did it to me" or "I couldn't help it" frame of mind. This frame of mind means we are trapped by how we perceive. We do not know that we have a choice to perceive differently because we assume that our perceptions are accurate. As a result we are fearful and we feel powerless. Feelings of powerlessness spawn a natural need to control people or situations that feel overwhelming. Being in control gives us a sense of power over situations and over people we might otherwise feel at the mercy of. The need to be in control is one of the many telltale signs that we are in *victim consciousness*.

There are other characteristics that define *victim consciousness*, including a tendency to denigrate ourselves. It is wise to become familiar with the signs and symptoms of *victim consciousness* (see the Signs of Victimhood eBook). The more quickly we perceive those telltale signs the more quickly we can free ourselves. Otherwise we limit our own potential and we limit our ability to perceive the potential in others. Limiting ourselves in these unhealthy ways leads to feeling mistreated by life and especially by those we have tried to help.

CHAPTER TWO

# Victim Perception and Its Opposite

When we are operating from *victim consciousness* we perceive the external world as the cause of anything and everything that happens in our lives. Living in *victim consciousness* we perceive ourselves as being at the mercy of reality. If we are going to cease living in that state we must shift our focus from an *externally oriented perception* to an *internally oriented perception*. We live our lives in either one or the other of these two ways of perceiving reality.

## *Two Basic Life Orientations*
These two opposing perceptions constitute two basic orientations to life:

1. Seeing life as determined by outside events beyond our control.
2. Seeing ourselves as responsible for our state of well-being or lack of well-being.

### The First Orientation: Limited Perception
When we consciously or unconsciously adopt the first orientation, we live as *victims* believing that the external world is the cause of everything that happens in our lives. We believe that we are controlled by external events. *Victim consciousness*, then, can be identified by this single primary orientation or criterion, and that orientation/criterion is, in turn, the identifying characteristic of *victim consciousness*. We constantly try to fix our problems by manipulating something out there. Instead of changing ourselves, we try to change other people's thoughts, beliefs, actions–an impossible task–and we judge and react accordingly.

What we don't realize is that we actually try to make others think as we do, believe as we do. We try to control others instead of ourselves, and when they refuse to be controlled, we are offended, we become angry, resentful, punishing, etc. We create our own misery, but because of our orientation to life, we believe others have created it. Not surprisingly, we experience frustration, we suffer, and we blame others for that frustration and suffering.

On the other hand, when we see the world through the second orientation, we understand that what we see in our daily lives is our own mental state being reflected back to us. This second orientation or frame of reference allows us to see that our own thoughts and beliefs create our struggles, biases, happiness/unhappiness, sense of success or lack thereof. This orientation or shift of mental consciousness sees the world as a kind place where we use our thoughts/beliefs to manage any challenges/struggles that present themselves. We learn to recognize that we, ourselves, are totally responsible for our inner peace and emotional well-being.

As a result, we are not judgmental or resistant to life; we are too busy making the internal adjustments necessary to improve the quality of our lives. We understand that the secret to having a good life is knowing that to find the source of pain or joy we must look, not outside to external matters, but within ourselves. As we shift from the first orientation to the second one, we move from living in a state of unhealthy and constant reaction to a state of positive and healthy creating. The second orientation is a state of consciousness that knows how to use what it sees to create and enhance our peace.

### The second orientation: expanded perception

If we are to shift from an *externally oriented perception* to an *internally oriented* one, we must begin to question the ideas and beliefs that cause us suffering.

For instance, from an *externally focused perception*, a lover leaves and we perceive the leaving as, "He/she abandoned me by walking away." But seeing the same thing from an *internally focused perspective* we might say something totally different, like, "It was time for him/her to go. By leaving, he/she did for me what I was not yet ready to do for myself; He/she left. Leaving was an act of love; it spared us both further pain."

It is important that we feel the energetic difference between these two statements which describe the same event: a lover leaving. Notice how much kinder the second set of statements are towards self and the other. These latter statements reflect a way of perceiving that helps us to accept a situation as it is and brings us peace. *Victim consciousness*, on the other hand, does not acknowledge acceptance and it does not value peace. It wants to protest. It wants to be right. *Victim consciousness* promotes *resistance* on every level.

To better understand how it is that our beliefs work to entrap us in *victim consciousness*, we need to examine a little deeper the nature of the energy of our thoughts and the influence that energy has on us.

# CHAPTER THREE

# The Energy Nature of Thoughts and Feelings

Energy is a compilation of molecules and atoms that are in perpetual motion even if we cannot see the motion. Only that which is alive can move and change, so it is fair to say that everything that is made up of atoms (all things are made up of atoms) is alive on some level.

If we move our hands through the space around us right now we may feel nothing. However, in reality, we move and breathe in a medium of molecules or of energy that is alive.

In the same way fish move and live in a water medium, we too are swimming in a sea of air, of energy that is alive (moving). I'm reminded of the story about the little fish who swam up to the big granddaddy fish and asked, "Grandpa, what is water?" We are like that little fish; we wander around in oblivion asking, "What is universal energy?" We fail to notice that we are being totally supported by the very stuff we neglect to acknowledge or are unaware of.

## Our Thoughts Generate Feelings

So, as science has demonstrated over and over, everything is made of moving atoms or living or vibrating energy. There are no exceptions. Everything is a form of vibrating energy whether it be our bodies, the chairs we are sitting on, the floor, earth, sky, stars, and on and on. The list is endless because it takes in all of creation. Thoughts and feelings are no exception. They are also a form of energy.

Because thoughts and feelings are also energy they vibrate, as do all forms of energy, at particular frequencies. Thoughts that vibrate at a *high-frequency* generate feelings of love, peace, enthusiasm, gratitude, joy, etc. whereas thoughts that vibrate at a *low-frequency* generate feelings of anxiety, anger, sadness, guilt, shame or depression. *Low-frequency* thoughts and emotion have a heavy, dense quality whereas *high-frequency* thoughts and feelings have a light and buoyant quality.

Indeed the mind acts like a generator cranking out thoughts. And when we believe what we think, our thoughts generate feelings. In other words, all of our feelings come from the thoughts we believe.

Positive, wholesome thoughts generate *high-frequency* feelings. Negative, critical thoughts generate *low-frequency* feelings. When our thoughts, for example, are peaceful and grateful, we feel "good." Similarly, when our thoughts are angry and judgmental, we feel "bad."

For instance if we believe the thought, "I am worthless," that belief generates feelings of unimportance, depression and inadequacy. If on the other hand, we believe the thought, "I am important," that belief generates feelings of significance and usefulness. The thoughts we believe determine our emotional well-being.

## *Our Feelings Determine Behavior*

Once we understand that emotion is generated by the nature and quality of our thoughts, it is easy to see that our behavior or how we act is governed by our feelings and thoughts. When we believe what we think, we feel and act accordingly. In other words, we necessarily "act out" our beliefs. No matter how well we may think we are hiding our feelings, denying them and/or bluffing, the truth remains that the thoughts and feelings they generate determine our actions and *reactions*.

Many of us use feelings as a guide in making decisions. If something feels good we assume we should do it. If we don't like the way something feels we assume we should avoid it. We don't realize that our feelings express *reactions* to our thoughts about the thing and not *reactions* to the thing.

Feelings were designed, not to tell us how to decide, but to alert us to the level of the *vibrational frequency* of our thoughts. Our feelings/emotions function much in the same way a gas gauge on the dashboard of our car works. The gas gauge simply reports how much gas there is in the tank; it does not fuel the car. In the same way, our feelings report to us the level of the *vibrational frequency* of our thoughts. When the gas gauge reads empty, we don't react in a panic, thinking we need to get rid of the car, or we need to throw a pill in the gas tank to "fix it," nor do we ignore the gauge and hope the problem will go away. We heed the signal by going to a gas station and putting gas in the tank.

Like a gas gauge on an automobile, our feelings inform us of the *vibrational frequency* of our thoughts. Such a "*frequency* report" allows us to adjust our thoughts and restore our emotional balance. When we understand the true function of our feeling nature, we no longer need to blame outside events. We are less likely to be consumed with the need to control our life situations; we no longer see external events as something that needs to be eliminated, changed or denied. Instead we use our feelings as messengers that show us when it's time to examine and adjust our thoughts and return to peace.

# Chapter Four

# Observer Consciousness
# Versus Victim Consciousness

In order to develop an *internally oriented perspective* and live in it, we must raise our emotional *vibrational frequency*. By doing so, we activate a part of ourselves known as *observer consciousness*. We all have an *observing* function; it is an inherent part of us. We are born with that ability but in many of us it has never been developed or if it has, it has atrophied from lack of use.

The *observer consciousness* sees *Reality* just as it is, that is, without judgment and without interpretation. It sees what actually is. *Observer consciousness* feels no need to deny, justify or make pretty what it sees because it does not judge *Reality* as right/wrong, good or bad. It simply *observes*. When we are in *observer consciousness,* we *witness* the relationship of cause and effect in our lives and in so doing we access our inner wisdom, that is, our inner knowing. *Observer consciousness* operates by registering facts in much the same way that an unbiased researcher might.

Without an active *observer consciousness* we aren't able to recognize when we are trapped in a *victim consciousness*. Accessing *observer consciousness* is not only a desirable goal, it is a necessary one. As a matter of fact, the *observer consciousness* is the antidote for *victim consciousness*.

Directly opposite from the *observer* function within our psyche is *victim consciousness*, often referred to as our ego, or *victim ego*. It is the complete antithesis of *observer consciousness* in quality and character. Whereas *observer consciousness* is detached and non-judgmental, the *victim ego* is *reactive* and *resistant*. It is that part of ourselves that perceives us as separate from the rest of the world. *Victim consciousness* creates stressful stories about how much we are at the mercy of life. It perceives the world through an externally focused lens, that of *victim consciousness.*

## A Nursery Rhyme Description of Victim Consciousness

"Peter, Peter, Pumpkin Eater" is the name of a nursery rhyme that aptly describes our relationship with *victim consciousness*: "Peter, Peter, Pumpkin Eater had a wife and couldn't keep her, so he put her in a pumpkin shell and there he kept her very well."

We can think of Peter Pumpkin Eater as *victim consciousness* and the wife he could not keep as our *observer consciousness.* The *observer consciousness* is the holy cup or grail that is penetrated by and filled with Spirit. It is our eternal essence and cannot truly be limited, although *victim consciousness* may convince us otherwise.

*Victim consciousness* (Peter Pumpkin Eater) imprisons our *observer consciousness* by restricting it to a pumpkin shell, a painfully limiting set of ideas, and then works to convince us that we are nothing more than that outer shell. *Victim consciousness*, in short, prevents us from knowing that we are, at our core, completely free and limitless.

Living in *victim consciousness* keeps us believing that we are a limited self, it rules us and misery reigns. We will go on living constricted lives. We must refuse to believe the limited definition of ourselves that *victim consciousness* promotes and realize that we are, in truth, much bigger than we imagine. When *victim consciousness* rules, we process everything we encounter through a *low-frequency* vibration or false mindset. Let us further define the term *victim consciousness* and explore how it develops.

## A Construct of Victim Consciousness

*Victim consciousness,* as the term is used here, refers to that part of us that is heavily invested in believing a negative, *low-frequency* definition of ourselves and the world. *Victim consciousness* consists of unceasing negative chatter that keeps us in a state of negative *reaction.*

To be more explicit, *victim consciousness* is an energy field created by negative mental thoughts that are strengthened and empowered by unhealthy beliefs. When we blindly believe these negative thoughts that come either from childhood wounds or are inherited from our family, we feel miserable; we create an unhappy self. The more we believe what are really unsubstantiated negative thoughts (although we believe we can substantiate them), the more we identify with *victim consciousness*. The latter is a part of every human being; we all have some degree of *victim consciousness*.

The term *victim consciousness* is synonymous with and can be used interchangeably with words and terms such as the personality, wounded child, persona, or any of the three roles on the *victim triangle*, (*persecutor, rescue*r or *victim)*, which I will introduce in detail later. (See pages 33-38.)

*Victim consciousness* is fueled by *low-frequency* thoughts, a statement which makes sense when we realize that *victim consciousness* came about in response to times in our early lives when we felt emotionally, mentally, or physically wounded. It lives on because we unconsciously reinforce negative beliefs adopted from a painful past. We believe the negative thoughts while at the same time we *resist* the painful emotions those thoughts create. Resistance of any form is food for *victim consciousness*.

Every time we believe *low-frequency* thoughts that generate unhappiness, *victim consciousness* grows. This explains why we are so often overtaken by it. It thrives on pain-producing drama and misunderstanding. It is the part of us that chooses to *react* painfully and perpetuate itself.

We need to better understand how it is that *victim consciousness* rules our lives so completely. *Victim consciousness* develops in three stages or aspects:

1. The original wound or trauma we experience,
2. The beliefs we create unconsciously about that event,
3. The *defenses* we gather to protect us from being wounded again.

Let's consider an illustration. Pretend we are witnessing the following scene: a small child (under the age of a year) is standing up in his baby bed, crying; he is totally distraught as he watches his parents yell and scream at each other in a full-fledged knock-down, drag-out fight.

The child is crying and very upset although he is not judging his parents about what should or shouldn't be happening. After all, he has nothing to compare it with, so how would he know any different? He doesn't know that there is anything unusual or wrong with what he is seeing. He is upset and has little, if any, understanding about why.

What he is feeling is the dense, heavy vibration of warring energy in the room created by the dueling parents. He feels the "wham" of a strong emotional charge that lands like a physical blow in his gut. Our little guy has no frame of reference for what is happening and therefore no way to understand or dissipate the heavy emotional charge that now settles, raw and unprocessed, in his psyche. What he feels is an example of the "original wound," and that experience illustrates the first stage in the development of *victim consciousness,* or the wounded self.

Now let's fast forward several years in this little boy's life. He is now age five or six and is still carrying that painful emotional charge although he has no memory of where it came from. Because he has no idea of its origin, he can't process it. Processing that initial wound/trauma is a necessity for releasing or freeing himself of its negative effects. The energy is now lodged in his psyche and becomes an emotional block.

As far as the child is concerned he has never NOT had this emotional blockage. He has carried this energy for as long as he can remember. There is no memory that the painful feelings relate to his parents' fighting; as far as he is concerned he has always had these inner painful feelings. He struggles to understand what he's dealing with and in so doing he creates an explanation of those feelings and their cause. He is the *victim*, of course; and his beliefs about what happened explains why he is the way he is. His rendition of what happened is, more often than not, a less than flattering explanation, full of limiting beliefs about himself and the world. He believes his explanation and it defines him and his relationship with the world. It is an explanation of himself as the wounded *victim*.

Because he is a unique individual, we cannot know for sure what he might think of himself. He might believe thoughts such as, "There's something wrong with me. I don't handle life well, I am strange, nobody else feels like I do, I am undeserving and not important"; or "People can't be trusted, they are dangerous and the world is a scary place"; or "Anger is bad, therefore I shouldn't feel angry."

What we can know is that because his beliefs come from wounded circumstances, they create a limiting and negative self-definition. He believes that definition of himself totally and without question! Because what he believes hurts, he feels forced to create *defensive* beliefs/behavior that protect him from other such wounds.

As was mentioned above, once the limited explanation that defines our hypothetical child is in place, his now almost fully formed *victim consciousness* develops its third stage: an arsenal of *defenses* meant to protect him from what he has come to perceive as a dangerous world.

Because he blindly believes his limited explanation about himself and life, he feels the need for protection. He needs a way to cover up the pain, or numb himself to it. And so he develops *defenses*. He has to justify his feelings/behavior, minimize them and/or compensate for, or control, his environment so he can feel safe.

We all have *defenses*. *Defenses* are a "knee-jerk" or negative reaction to something we perceive to be a potential or perceived attack. *Defenses* generally work against us rather than for us. Rather than preventing further pain, they reinforce and perpetuate our negative beliefs about life, creating more unhappiness and drama for us instead of keeping us safe.

The following are some common examples of *defense* strategies: "I won't expect or need anything from anyone"; "I'll take care of myself"; "I won't get close to people so they won't see how unworthy I am"; "I will keep people distant so they can't hurt me";

"I will strike out first before they get me"; "I will earn their respect by being perfect"; "I will pretend I don't care"; "I will do everything for them so they will need me."

In summary then, *victim consciousness* originates out of some kind of early childhood wounding that we may not consciously remember but from which we still carry emotional baggage. We continue to create and sustain a painfully, limiting definition of ourselves based on the emotional baggage we carry, replete with *defense* strategies for self-protection. At some point this conglomeration of wounded energy, limiting beliefs, and protective *defenses* come together to form the identity of a *victim self, or victim consciousness.*

For most of us, it is *victim consciousness* that is in charge of our thinking. As we grew up, we saw *victim consciousness* modeled by everyone we knew. We watched most of our family and friends react out of unconscious thinking, thinking that was not closely examined and evaluated for accuracy or for its effect on themselves and others. It is out of such unconscious thinking that *victim consciousness* originates.

*Victim consciousness* can be summed up by a simple formula developed by renowned author Byron Katie (2002): We think a thought, we believe the thought, we act as if that belief is true and then we set about proving it (www.thework.com).

For example, if we believe the thought, "I am a bad person," we will act the part. We will act in thoughtless, painful ways that will verify that belief. When we believe these kinds of painful thoughts, we create for ourselves a *personal reality* that is steeped in *victim consciousness.*

*Victim consciousness* is founded on the sort of distorted reactive thinking that comes from blindly believing everything we think. It is *victim consciousness* that prompts us to *react* defensively and that keeps us in *victim consciousness. Victim consciousness* can then be defined as that state of consciousness we create for ourselves when we believe distorted, limiting thoughts and act them out. It is *victim consciousness* that generates these negative thoughts and prompts us to act like *victims.* In *victim consciousness*, we unconsciously react in ways that teach others how to treat us; it teaches them to treat us according to our own limited perception of ourselves. That limited perception keeps us living in a *low-frequency* state of *victim consciousness*.

Thinking about thoughts and feelings as energy with a particular *frequency* makes sense because all energy forms vibrate. Just as a vibrating string produces a certain sound on a musical instrument, our thoughts, too, vibrate and produce particular emotions. The level at which our thoughts vibrate determines the kind and quality of the emotions we experience.

As we mentioned earlier, our emotional energy moves between two basic frequencies: high and low. *High-frequency* thoughts are ones that align us with *Reality* and a sense of peace. They engender good feelings like love, acceptance, joy, patience, and gratitude. *Low-frequency* thoughts are stress producing and generate feelings of resistance like anxiety, resentment, guilt, doubt, anger. We think of these feelings as "bad." Most of us have a particular set of *low-frequency* beliefs that keep us from a life of joy and acceptance. These beliefs arise from our original wounding experiences and the subsequent explanations we created about ourselves and the world. We call these *low-frequency* and limiting thoughts *core beliefs*.

CHAPTER FIVE

# Core Beliefs As Energy

## *Core Beliefs Create an Electromagnetic Energy*

Again, the thoughts we believe and the feelings generated by those beliefs attract to us other thoughts of a similar *vibrational frequency*. The belief "I am worthless" brings a multitude of corresponding thoughts to support that belief as a basic or core idea. It has a *low-frequency*. Substantiating thoughts such as, "I can't do it right, I'm a failure, I don't matter, they don't like me, I don't deserve happiness," vibrate at a similarly *low-frequency* and therefore might well revolve around and support a central theme of worthlessness.

All of us have at least a few central or *core* beliefs. These core beliefs can be healthy and/or unhealthy and prompt and govern our actions throughout life. (From here on, whenever I refer to core beliefs, I mean unhealthy core beliefs.) These *core beliefs* act like an electromagnetic center attracting to us a whole bevy of beliefs with a similar *frequency*, beliefs that reinforce our central theme.

Eventually a whole personality is created out of this bevy of homogenous beliefs about ourselves and the world. These supporting beliefs are held in place by the electromagnetic pull of our central or *core beliefs*.

Let's look at a rather common scenario: a person we will call Jody has a central theme: "I have to be the best at everything or I don't matter." Once she becomes aware of that *core belief*, she begins to notice how her life is saturated with supporting beliefs that reinforce that theme. In her marriage, the theme shows up in her highly charged and competitive interaction with her husband. She constantly compares herself to him ("I have to win, be right and in charge") and judges him ("you're stupid, inferior, or unappreciative of me"). She relentlessly criticizes herself too ("I have to be perfect and I'm not. I'm a fake and a failure"). Jody even notices that her *core beliefs* determine the way she interacts with strangers. She sees everyone she knows as either blocking her progress or not worth the bother. She is constantly engaged in either a one-up or a one-down relationship with others simply because she believes the thought, "I do not count unless I am the best." That latter statement is an example of a *core belief.*

A *core belief,* then, is a decision about ourselves or the world that is most often made unconsciously and even pre-verbally. It is a deeply personal and unquestioned idea about who we are and what we can expect from the world. *Core beliefs* function just below the level of consciousness. Acting much like a subliminal tape recording, these vibrational energies circulate nonstop and they have a powerful effect on us. Many of our daily life decisions and choices are determined by their magnetic pull.

By visualizing that nucleus of *low-frequency core beliefs* as an electromagnetic energy field that attracts to it a whole bevy of similar and supporting beliefs, we can better understand how *core beliefs* influence our minds. *Core beliefs* come together around a centralized belief to form a tightly woven identity that defines us and determines what we need to do to survive in the world as we perceive it. Even though our *core beliefs* generate misery, we adopt this limited definition of ourselves and then we live it out as if it were true. We act it out in often painful and unhappy ways.

The definition that we adopt as the truth about who we are takes on a life of its own while we are still quite young. By the age of five most of us have a fully formed definition of who we are and what we can expect from life. Such a crystalized identity of self with its own distinct set of characteristics is what we commonly refer to as our personality.

Our personality consists of both our *core beliefs* (healthy or unhealthy) as well as the *defenses* and supports we develop around those beliefs. We create those supporting or secondary beliefs as *defenses* to protect and help us cope with a world we have created based on the negative or positive stories we have come to believe. When our *core beliefs* are unhealthy, much of the misery we experience results from the secondary beliefs we have that defend the unhealthy *core beliefs*.

For instance, Angie realized a core theme in her family was a belief that happiness is dangerous and leads to loss and grief. "If I am too happy, somebody will pay." She believed that anytime she dared to enjoy her life she was punished somehow, usually through the loss (by death or divorce) of a loved one. Not surprisingly, she developed beliefs that caused her to avoid intimacy and engage in self destructive behavior. She felt the need to protect herself from a world that she believed would punish her for being happy. Clearly, Angie's energy field was painfully limited; she created a personality or painful energy field out of a false set of *core beliefs*.

## Negative Core Beliefs Verified

We do what we do because we believe what we believe. Our behavior is determined by what we believe. This is always true because behavior follows belief. We can't do anything else! As long as we go on blindly believing what we tell ourselves, we will act accordingly.

We unconsciously live out whatever negative identity or limiting definition of ourselves we believe, whether it is one of limitation, failure, abuse, or constant life struggle. In so doing, we verify or prove true our beliefs. If we think we are unlovable, for instance, we will act in unlovable ways and alienate others. We then use their negative response towards us as evidence for our negative opinion of ourselves.

As we stated earlier, how we experience the world depends on the *vibrational frequency* of our thoughts. *Low-frequency* thoughts attract *low-frequency* events/*reactions* whereas *higher frequency* thoughts set us on a *frequency path* that manifests in more positive life experiences.

We transmit a personal *frequency* and "broadcast" it, similar to the way a radio station broadcasts a particular radio show. For instance, we cannot access our favorite country music station by tuning in to NPR, no matter how hard we try. We have to tune in to the right wavelength. In a similar fashion, because our thoughts determine our *emotional frequency,* we can only transmit energy from the vibrational range of our thoughts. What we encounter and what we attract resonate at the *vibrational frequency* of our thoughts.

Our daily life faithfully reports to us the *vibrational frequency* of our current thoughts or beliefs. We cannot experience a *high-frequency* life if we believe and *react* from *low-frequency* thoughts. Our thoughts must generate a *frequency* that is compatible with what we want. We have to *align* with our desires if we are to manifest them. Because how we *react* to life depends on our thoughts about it, we will go on harvesting *low-frequency* thoughts until we *align* with *higher frequency* ones.

Perhaps the most difficult thoughts to recognize, our *core beliefs,* are those that did not originate out of our own life experience, but came down to us from our family. Such *core beliefs* are difficult to recognize because we have lived with them so long we fail to notice their negative impact upon us. We don't question these family beliefs; we simply assume they are true. We inherit them; they may be generations old!

Long before we arrived, our parents were living out of their established beliefs about life. Such beliefs consist of unquestioned ideas about who our family is, how worthy we are, what the world is like and what we can expect from life. We blindly take on these ideas as our own without examining them. And if our parents hold these ideas, we believe they must be true.

Take a hypothetical example: Joan and her brother Joe were unhappy with their lives and decided to attend a *core belief* workshop together and explore their family beliefs. They agreed that their family operated from beliefs that sounded something like the following: "It's us against the world. Life is hard and people are always trying to take advantage of us so we have to constantly watch our backs. We can only trust each other and our closest family members, and sometimes we can't trust all family members!"

Joan and Joe each got in touch with how their personal beliefs had evolved out of a set of family beliefs. Further exploring revealed that their family history was fraught with examples of how those family beliefs had been lived by their parents, aunts, uncles and grandparents. These family beliefs made up a life view that had dominated their family tree for generations, bringing scarcity, distrust, paranoia and much anxiety.

It had never once occurred to either of them to question the thoughts associated with their family's beliefs! They had simply lived their lives with the assumption that the view of the world that they had inherited from their family was accurate. As a result, they unconsciously acted in ways that perpetuated and verified that view. They continued to live in emotional pain until they got weary of it and decided to do something about it.

Not all family beliefs are pain-producing ones of course. There are some wonderful life-affirming beliefs that come down to us from our family, beliefs that we, in turn, pass on to our children. A family belief, for instance, that says we are a bright and successful family is not one we need to concern ourselves about. It is not the empowering beliefs we need to question. It is the misery-generating beliefs that need to be recognized and addressed because instead of keeping us safe, they create more unhappiness and drama for us.

It is important to notice our beliefs and the *frequencies/vibrations* they produce. If they make us unhappy, we cannot make positive changes until we know the source of our disharmony. As we examine our unhappy beliefs we learn that it is *victim consciousness* that generates pain because that's what *victim consciousness* does. The wounded self that engages in *victim consciousness* is addicted to *low-frequency* thoughts/beliefs that *resist* life and the result is *low-frequency* feelings. *Victim consciousness* is the source of most, if not all, of the emotional pain we experience.

### Negative Core Beliefs Projected

*Victim consciousness* is strengthened by creating and projecting negative beliefs, and it feeds on the resulting *low-frequencies*. It then projects those frequencies onto others and to life in general to justify the belief that we are *victims* of an unfair world. *Victim consciousness resists* change. It controls our psyches by forcing us to *react* out of negative/limiting beliefs.

*Victim consciousness* insists on being right! Of course, it is impossible to always be right. But to constantly need to justify one's position requires effort, denial, and mental strain. When we are in *victim consciousness,* we love to be against something or someone, to see others as being wrong, to *resist* what is, because that is how *victim consciousness* justifies and strengthens itself.

By *projecting* limiting beliefs onto others and to what is, we remain in a *low-frequency* state of judgment, unhappiness, and pain; we are in *victim consciousness.* Meanwhile, our authentic selves shrivel from negligence. In *victim consciousness,* we *resist* expressions of authenticity; we *resist Reality.*

When *victim consciousness* dominates us with negative thinking and painful beliefs, we inevitably *resist Reality.* Anytime we *resist Reality* with thoughts about how things should or shouldn't be, we can be sure that *victim consciousness* is in charge.

Once *victim consciousness* securely embeds itself in our thinking, prompting us to live out our *core beliefs* through our *reactions* to life, we automatically do the next natural thing: we *project* those thoughts/beliefs onto a situation or person who can then play the part needed to verify those thoughts/beliefs.

*Projection* is defined in the online Google dictionary as follows, "Projection: the unconscious transfer of one's own desires or emotions on to another." I suggest the addition of the word, *core beliefs* to the list of what's possible to *project* on to others, thus modifying that definition in part: " ... the unconscious transfer of one's own *core beliefs*, desires or emotions on to another."

A good analogy is to think of the mind as a movie projector which, as we know, *projects* film on to a blank screen. In our analogy, the film represents our own *core beliefs* which are finessed into a potent drama. That potent drama is rehearsed so much that we lose touch with our *authentic self.*

The empty screen symbolizes our daily world minus our *core beliefs*. The world, like an empty screen, simply awaits our next *projection*. It provides a neutral background for the drama we *project*, and we will *project*; it's what we do!

Humans cannot stop *projecting* thoughts, nor would we really want to stop *projecting* them, once we learn how to operate our minds/thoughts/beliefs in a healthier way! When we understand how the human mind collaborates with universal truths (such as those presented here), then we are able to use mental tools, such as *projection*, for our highest good. What we see in the world around us is really what we *project*: the reflection of our mind-generated *beliefs*. The world does not act upon us. It does not create our beliefs, any more than a film actually creates what we see at the movies. Our mind, like a projector, is the real source of the images we see on this screen called life!

When we *project* our beliefs onto another, we throw out a sort of fishing net, or web of energy that is designed to capture evidence for our particular *core beliefs*. When the *beliefs* we *project* onto another is a *low-frequency* web of energy, such as, "He is trying to hurt me, he can't be trusted," then we can reasonably expect a *low-frequency*, or negative response.

If we believe a person is trying to hurt us and can't be trusted, then we behave toward that person accordingly. We *react* in a negative, *defensive* manner. And it shouldn't come as a surprise then when the person, in turn, *reacts* in a way that reinforces our *core belief* and thus our painful drama. The person picks up on our *low-frequency* and *reacts* accordingly.

In the same way a dog picks up on our fear and *reacts* by growling or snapping at us, others too, pick up on our emotional energy field and automatically react to the behavioral cues we unconsciously send them. Their response proves to us that what we believe is absolutely true! The primary goal of *victim consciousness* (to be right) is thus achieved!

What we see, then, is always what we *project* because we can only see what we believe or think to be true. We cannot see anything other than what we decide is true because it hasn't occurred to us to look beyond the perimeters of our beliefs/thoughts. As a result, much of the time, we settle for a severely limited belief system that creates much unhappiness.

I remember reading in an old history book an anecdote that serves as a great example to illustrate how strong our *projections* can be. The anecdote is about the *reactions* of the Australian aborigines when they encountered Captain Cook, in 1770, for the first time. The Europeans sailed into the aborigines' harbor from an open sea and it was the first time the natives had ever seen ships and white men. That these strangers (white men) came out of the sea seemed even more astounding to the natives because they had not yet conceived of the possibility that such things as ships existed. These bearded strangers seemed to be gods who had come up from the watery depths of the sea. The astonishing and interesting part of this historical account is that the natives could not see the ships in the harbor! The Europeans pointed and gesticulated towards the ships, showing the natives through pantomime how they had come to their land; they even drew images of the ships in the sand, but the natives only guffawed because they could not see the ships.

Finally the sailors took the head chief and a few other natives out to the ship in their rowboat, but it was not until the rowboat came right up to the caption's ship that the mental spell that had kept them from seeing the ships broke, and the natives, sat in the rowboat and stared in complete amazement at the sight of "huge objects suddenly appearing from out of nowhere!"(Hambling, 2007).

The natives had not been pretending that they did not see the ships. They, very literally, could not see the ships! The ships were invisible to them, even though those ships were anchored only a small distance from the shoreline where they all stood. They could not see the ships because they did not believe in ships. They had never seen a floating vessel the size of a ship and so had no concept of how such a thing could possibly exist.

The aborigines were *projecting* their beliefs, as all humans do. We see only what we believe. Nothing more and nothing less. Even though what we see is always our *projection*, most of us will ask, yet again, "But suppose what I am seeing is not just my *projection?* What if they really are doing what I believe they are doing? The people and situations we attract into our lives match our vibrations/*frequencies*/beliefs. After all, we unconsciously hand-pick them for the job! *Projection* works because, as human story-makers, we unconsciously pick the perfect someone who fits the role we need to have played. In *victim consciousness,* we unconsciously scan the crowd until we find someone whose *frequency* matches the *frequency* of our beliefs, and then we feel justified in *projecting* our beliefs onto that person.

Often, the recipients of our *projection* share beliefs similar to our own, or they may have complementary *core beliefs* that make it easy for us to *project* our beliefs. In other words, we unconsciously pick someone who is a fit, meaning they have several characteristics that qualify them for the role we are casting them in. That role is to adequately embody our *projections.*

What we see in others justifies our *projection*: "He really does drink like an alcoholic; it's not just my opinion!" It is vital to remember that what he does is not nearly as important as what my mind does with what he is doing; what matters is our thoughts about the behavior, not the behavior itself. *Victim consciousness* inevitably prompts me to judge him, to fix him, or to control him. But my job is not to judge him or fix him but to question my beliefs about his behavior. Such an approach leaves me free to challenge my limiting thoughts and move towards *Reality* and peace.

When we have strong feelings towards others, either positive or negative, we can be assured that those others are in our lives for a reason. Their *vibrational frequency* is a match for some part of ourselves that, through *projection*, we are being given the opportunity to see. The way they interact with us is not by coincidence.

Our interaction with others is designed to trigger our unconscious beliefs and bring them to our awareness. These people serve the purpose of mirroring to us the beliefs we need to explore. Every person in our life serves, either in a positive or negative way, as a mirror for us. We *project* our opinion or belief on them, and thus we can make that piece of our belief system conscious. How else are we going to see what we believe except through such *projection*?

The people who trigger resentment, angst, guilt, or fear in us are the ones we would do well to *observe* most closely! The important question to ask ourselves when we feel uncomfortably triggered by another is, "What is it I most *resist* about this person? What am I telling myself about their behavior? What are the beliefs/feelings underlying my thoughts?"

By asking ourselves questions such as these we are able to reel in our *projections*, at least to some degree. We are able to locate and question the beliefs we *project* onto others. By identifying and clearing our *projections*, we have more direction over our responses to life. Rather than blindly *reacting* from painful *core beliefs*, we learn to *observe* and question what we believe, remembering that our beliefs are the true source of our happiness/unhappiness.

In summary, *victim consciousness* causes our unhappiness. We are unhappy when we believe the unverified, *low-frequency* beliefs created by *victim consciousness* and then *project* them onto the world. Again, remember that the *victim consciousness* promotes negative thoughts/beliefs to generate the *resistance* it needs to sustain itself.

CHAPTER SIX

# Core Beliefs and the Victim Triangle

Unhappy beliefs/programming we inherit from our families and the resulting negative thoughts we blindly accept drive us from one role to another on the *victim triangle*. These painfully limiting beliefs cause our unhappiness and establish a particular pattern or *victim* role out of which we automatically react. It is our *core beliefs* that hold us captive and constitute a *victim* energy field in which we live, think, and act. That energy field is best illustrated by the *victim triangle*.

Within that energy field, we and those to whom we relate/play out the roles of *victim, rescuer,* and *persecutor,* roles that verify and validate our life limiting stories. We seldom realize that we are unconsciously acting out a painful personal drama made up of *core beliefs* that come down to us from a family lineage we never doubt or question, but that is exactly what we do. Through the three roles found on the *victim triangle* we verify our own *core beliefs*.

## *A Review Of The Victim Triangle*
We may recall that the state of *victim consciousness* constitutes three major roles that we take turns shuffling through, roles that serve to perpetuate that state. These three roles were first diagrammed on a downward-facing triangle in the nineteen-seventies by <u>Dr. Stephen Karpman, Ph.D</u>, a well known practitioner of Transactional Analysis; the downward facing triangle is called "The Drama Triangle." (I call it the *victim triangle* because no matter where we are on the triangle we are in *victim consciousness*.) I have taken Dr. Karpman's basic and profound concept of "The Drama Triangle" and its three positions (*persecutor, rescuer,*

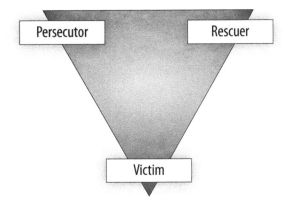

and *victim*) and further defined them into, what I call, *starting gate positions* that have unique *core beliefs* and distinct characteristics that identify each role. "The Drama Triangle" (*victim triangle*) has been an important part of my work with clients since I was introduced to it in the seventies. I consider it to be an essential tool in helping us to understand (and simplify) the complexities of *victim consciousness* and free us from it.

The *victim triangle* is an inverted one. Dr. Karpman defined the three roles positioned on his "The Drama Triangle" as the *rescuer,* the *persecutor,* and the *victim.* We might call these three roles the three faces of *victim consciousness.* At the bottom point of the inverted triangle we find the central *victim* role, the role we return to over and again. Both the *rescuer* and *persecutor* are on the top ends of the *triangle* in a one-up relationship to the *victim* position at the bottom.

Sitting at opposite corners from each other at the top of the *triangle,* the roles of *rescuer* and *persecutor* are the two extreme expressions of *victim consciousness.* The *victim* role gets a proverbial crick in the neck from always looking up at these two roles which consider themselves superior to the *victim* role.

Because of its lowly position on the *triangle,* the *victim* role fosters feelings of being inferior. These feelings, in turn, spark a dark resentment in the *victim* towards the other two roles (*rescuer* or *persecutor*) which the *victim* perceives as superior to it.

*Guiding Principles for Life*

Not surprisingly, such festering resentment may prompt the person playing the *victim* role to move up into the *persecutor* role in search of ways to get even.

And the rotation around the *victim triangle* begins and for some, never stops. We spend most of our time moving from one role to another on the *victim triangle* at home, at work, and even with our best friends. The *victim triangle* is so named mainly because whether or not we start out being *persecutors* or *rescuers* we always feel like *victims*. For many of us, interacting from one of the three roles on the *victim triangle* is the only style of relating we know.

**Starting Gate Positions on the Victim Triangle**
Even though we change roles on the *victim triangle* every time we are on it, we also have what I call a *starting gate position* on the triangle. The *starting gate position* is the role that we most often identify with and it is the role we often get hooked into playing first.

Each *starting gate position* has its own particular way of perceiving the world based on beliefs that support that particular role. *Starting gate rescuers,* for instance, tend to believe that their own personal needs are irrelevant. They believe that they matter only when they are taking care of others, and that means they constantly need someone to take care of.

*Starting gate persecutors* believe the world is generally an unsafe and fearful place. They think of themselves as being in constant need of protection from a world that is out to get them and so they get angry at others or at situations believing they are only defending themselves.

*Starting gate victims* think of themselves as weak and unable to take care of themselves and so they are constantly on the lookout for someone to rescue them.

Each *starting gate position* has its own way of moving around the *victim triangle*, a way that is unique to how it perceives the world. Let's take a look at one example to demonstrate how one role, a *rescuer* in this case, might move around the *victim triangle*.

Sue's *starting gate position* is that of the *rescuer* and like all true *rescuers* she believes that her personal needs and wants are unimportant. She believes that she matters to others only if she takes really good care of them. Because Sue believes such thoughts, she unconsciously looks for people who need to be taken care of (*victims*) and then *rescues* them as a way to feel important. She ends up fostering dependency on herself among those she takes care of. She stays stuck on the *victim triangle* by first *rescuing* others and then *persecuting* them and or herself when she feels unappreciated. In other words, Sue the *rescuer* becomes a *persecutor* because she feels like a *victim*. Such is the way a *starting gate rescuer* moves around the *triangle*.

The *victim triangle* with its three faces (*victim, rescuer, persecutor*) is the playing field upon which all dysfunctional interaction takes place. It is our main playing field when we live in *victim consciousness*. To be stuck in such a limited, unhappy state means that we have an *externally focused orientation* to life. When we see the world as being separate from us and/or perceive ourselves as being victimized by what's outside of us, we are perceiving life from an *externally oriented perspective*. We assume this perspective is the only way to see *Reality* but it is not. There is an *internally focused orientation,* or way of perceiving, that is much kinder and certainly more realistic.

## An Example: Paula's Core Beliefs On The Victim Triangle
To demonstrate how a *core belief* might be played out on the *victim triangle*, let's explore a case example. Paula's *core belief* says she is unworthy. Her supporting cast of reinforcing beliefs include thoughts like, "No one could possibly love me, therefore I will be rejected. They only want me for what I can do for them," and, "Being close to people is dangerous. I need to be suspicious of their motives and hold them at a distance."

Such thoughts establish an energy field that dictates Paula's behavior. All of her interaction with others is guided and influenced by these thoughts. Paula automatically acts so that others will feel justified in behaving towards her in ways that verify those *core beliefs* that say she is unworthy. In other words, she interacts with others in ways that ask for a negative response. Though she is unaware of it, her behavior elicits a *low-frequency,* hurtful *reaction* from others in keeping with the *low-frequency* thoughts she is thinking. She then uses that hurtful *reaction* to reinforce her own limiting beliefs about herself. Her whole life is lived within a *low-frequency* energy field of her own making. She has no idea that she, herself, is creating that energy field.

For instance, Paula is unhappy with her boyfriend because she says, "He is cold and rejecting of me." When asked to describe her own behavior in the relationship, it becomes clear that her *core beliefs* create conflicting and contradictory feelings and messages.

One minute she sees herself as needy and wanting his total attention. (She is in the *victim* role on the *victim triangle.*) The next minute, she acts cold and withdrawn toward him, pushing him away (she is now in the *persecutor* role). Her behavior/responses toward her boyfriend depends on what she is currently telling herself about their relationship. It is no wonder that he reacts by pulling away!

Whenever Paula pursues Ted from a place of neediness and demands his attention, he retreats, prompting Paula to feel victimized by his withdrawal (because she sees him as a *persecutor*). Sometimes this behavior goes on for days. She often becomes sullen and cold; he gets angry and even more distant, thus proving to Paula that her beliefs are true. She moves from being a *victim* to being a *persecutor,* to again being a *victim*, and that just serves to reinforce her limiting *core beliefs* about herself.

When the distance between them gets too painful, Paula does something extra special for Ted, usually in the form of *rescuing* (she moves into the *rescuer* role on the *victim triangle*). For example, she might make his car payment when he is in arrears. In so doing, she fosters his dependence on her. The more she *rescues* him the more resentful and less appreciated she feels. Whether she plays the role of *rescuer* or *persecutor*, underneath she always feels like a *victim*.

Of course, Ted is in *victim consciousness* as well. Their relationship consists of a painful repetition of neediness, rejection (*victim*), *rescuing, (rescuer)* resentment, and striking out (*persecutor*) from a place of feeling hurt. Because of their beliefs about each other's thoughts and actions, Paula and Ted prove to each other over and over that no one can possibly love them. Paula believes that the only way for her to keep a boyfriend is to *rescue* him. Ted also believes that the only way he can keep a girlfriend is to, in turn, *rescue* her.

To move out of *victim consciousness* and off of the *victim triangle*, both Paula and Ted must discover their *core beliefs* and question them. They, like us, must learn how to separate unhappy beliefs from the truth, from *Reality*. To do that they need, and we need, to explore the nature of *Reality*.

# CHAPTER SEVEN

# Alignment with Reality and Source

Reality is what is; it is the bare-bone facts of the events that are either currently unfolding before our eyes or that have already happened. *Reality* can never happen in the future and our recollection of *Reality* in the past tense is altered, or contaminated, by our interpretation of it. If we cannot hear, see, touch, taste or smell it, then what we are perceiving is not *Reality* at all, but is instead, our beliefs about *Reality*.

But even our senses can sometimes deceive us when it comes to reporting *Reality* as was illustrated in the account about natives having their first experience with a sailing ship (p.30). In *Reality* the ships were there within plain view, but because the natives did not believe in such things, they could only experience *Reality* according to their beliefs. They, therefore, could not experience the *Reality* of floating vessels on the water. Beliefs can be so powerful that they can alter our sensory experience of *Reality*! For that reason, it is wise to question our perceptions.

We can make a commitment to anchor in the *Reality* of this moment. The present moment is the source of *highest frequency* that can be found. The present moment contains the healing energy of a Universal *Source* that cannot be accessed through a past or future orientation (Tolle, Eckhart, 1999). Past and future are places that do not exist except in a confused mind. *Reality* is the place where peace waits and peace is always available for us in the present moment, or what Eckhart Tolle calls the *NOW*.

Most of us have heard the expression "There are no mistakes." This expression states a universal truth gleaned from the "Law of Cause and Effect": every cause has its effect;

every effect has its cause; everything happens according to Law; chance is but a name for Law not recognized; there are many planes of causation, but nothing escapes the Law." (The Kybalion; A Study of The Hermetic Philosophy of Ancient Egypt and Greece, by The Three Initiates, 1912).

Everything, person or event, we encounter, is the way it is for a reason. Nothing arises out of mere happenstance. When we apply the *Law of Cause and Effect* to our lives, we recognize that what we see and experience is, and will always be, a reflection of our own beliefs! The world is a mirror, literally! It mirrors to us our own inner mental state. Knowing and accepting that is the secret to understanding how everything that happens in our lives is happening *for* us, rather than *to* us. We are not *victims* of circumstance, but co-creators of our *personal reality*.

However, when we *resist Reality* we see a world full of accidental happenings, mistakes and coincidences. When we *resist* what is, we are frustrated because what's happening isn't how we think things should be; life is not happening according to our plans. As a result we are unhappy. We are in *victim consciousness*.

When we see life as problematic, it is because we are not living in the merciful, generous, and loving present, but in a mind-created hell of our own making. When we *react* to outside events with negative thoughts/beliefs/stories, we can know that our *victim consciousness* is *resisting* what is. The resulting *low-frequency* feelings, triggered by our response to those outside events, indicate clearly that we are resisting *Reality, Source,* and peace.

On the other hand, when we are truly *aligned* with *Reality*, we know there are no mistakes. We understand that what we see is always a reflection of our own beliefs. This *Reality* check helps us to see our beliefs for what they are: peace-making beliefs or misery-making beliefs. The "*Reality* check" is really a "*Source* check." Are we aligned with *Reality/Source* (peace) or are we *resisting* it (pain/misery)?

Through *Reality*, we have an opportunity to converse with a Living Intelligence, or *Source*. Let's look at the following analogy: Imagine *Source* as light itself (much like the sun, which is often used to symbolize higher consciousness) that shines into the depths of our mind. Now imagine that our own limiting beliefs are blocking the way so that the light of consciousness cannot fully penetrate to our core. It cannot fully enlighten us. As a result, we do not allow ourselves to be what we truly are, emanations (like rays of the sun) of that brilliant *Source*.

However, even though our connection may be obstructed, *Source* cannot be stopped from shining, just as clouds may block the sunlight but cannot prevent the sun from shining. And because *Source* wants to fully merge with us, it continues to shine directly on the thought or belief that obstructs its path. Moreover, the mental belief that stands between us and *Source* is energetically *projected* out in physical form as a shadow of our *resistance*. Such *projected* shadows alert us to our limiting beliefs, and we can choose to change them. What a demonstration of the love and desire of *Source* to reconnect with us! We can consciously reconnect with *Source* in each moment, in the *NOW*.

*Reality* is always working for us. *Reality*, even when it brings hardship, brings into our lives through *Source* exactly what we need to remind us that we are the beloved emanations of *Source* Itself.

## Adjusting Our Emotional Frequency

Unconditional love is the energy of *Source* and it is the highest vibrational frequency possible. *Aligning* with *Source* energy requires that we adjust our emotional frequency from that of the *victim's* vibration to one that more closely matches the vibration of unconditional love.

We *align* with such a high vibration by replacing our *low-frequency* beliefs with thoughts that produce a more positive, *higher frequency*. Thoughts of gratitude and acceptance, for instance, elevate our frequency, bringing us closer to *Source*, whereas thoughts that produce jealousy or resentment lower our frequency and separate us further from the unconditional love of *Source*. We cannot attain *high-frequency* states of consciousness as long as we operate out of a *low-frequency* or *victim consciousness*. Therefore, if we want to experience a higher quality of life we must engage in a *frequency adjustment.* A *frequency adjustment* occurs when we directly and incrementally shift our negative states of consciousness to higher states.

When we *align* with the unconditional love of *Source*, we experience a more positive quality of life. Our higher emotional frequency then attracts to our lives what we desire. When we feel good, when we are at peace, when we are accepting, congruent, or grateful, our emotional body is reporting that we are in *alignment* with what is - *Reality/Source.* Whereas when we experience any level of unhappiness, our emotional body is telling us that our thinking is out of *alignment.*

The emotional body has two functions. It signals us when we are in or out of *alignment* with *Source.* It also transmits our *vibrational frequency* so that people and events with a similar vibration are drawn to us. In much the same way that a radio sends out sound frequencies, our emotional body signals the *frequency path* upon which we travel. Life events thus come together to match our frequency, and in this way we create our *personal reality.*

Let's say, for instance, that a woman believes all men are angry and abusive. Because of that belief, she unconsciously transmits a negative emotional vibration about men. Not surprisingly, she finds herself attracted to a man who typifies her negative belief!

Our thoughts/beliefs produce the emotional energy which, in turn, electromagnetically attracts the life situation that will match the *frequency* of those thoughts/beliefs. We can, however, benefit from this knowledge by learning how to create for ourselves a protective shield of positive energy.

If we are traveling and believe that we are safe, we have created around us, because of that belief, a *bubble of protection* made up of *high-frequency* energy. If on the other hand, we tell ourselves (and believe) that traveling is always difficult and that people are unkind mercenaries who look for ways to take advantage of us, then we have created a *frequency path* that will attract what we believe: our wallet is lifted in the line at the amusement park, our rental car is broken into, and/or we encounter suspiciously acting people everywhere we go.

Surrounding ourselves, our loved ones, and valuable possessions with positive beliefs creates a highly effective *bubble of protection*. Our mother may have taught us when we were children to
surround ourselves with such a bubble whenever we worried about
something getting stolen. For instance, my mother would encourage me and my siblings to visualize our school bags or favorite
toys in a bubble of safety. She then told us to say a brief prayer of
thanks for the protection and trust that it would be so.

A prayer of thanks is an important part of the *bubble of protection* formula because it allows us to stop worrying and adjust our
*low-frequency* thinking to a *higher frequency* of gratitude; such
mental adjustment is a key part of attracting protection.

The *bubble of protection* works for those of us who practice
using it. We can apply it anytime we find ourselves fretting over
the safety of children, friends, our homes, treasured possessions,
or ourselves.

The *bubble of protection* is an example of how we can direct, or
focus energy. To create it, we use intention, attention, visualization and gratitude. We also use the same tools to transform *victim
consciousness*. To shift out of *victim consciousness*, we must first
intend to make the shift and then we attend to our mental energy/
thoughts/beliefs.

There is a universal law that observes the following meta-
physical fact: whatever we pay attention to grows. It doesn't
matter whether we focus on something in a negative or in a
positive way, it is attention that empowers and increases that
upon which we focus. Our *attention* promotes expansion because it is through attention that we direct and focus universal
energy. We might say that our ability to focus, i.e. to direct our
attention, creates a fertilizing action.

A good gardener pays careful attention to his garden. Every
day he observes what plants need watering, what plants need
pruning, and he notices the overall health of each plant. In
other words, he pays attention to his garden; he attends to it. As
a result, the garden thrives and produces abundance.

In a similar way, our attention fertilizes our personal garden - our lives. The kind of life we have depends on what we choose to focus on. Important questions to ask are, "What kind of life do I want to cultivate?"; "Am I cultivating a life of negative beliefs (weeds) or a life of positive beliefs (healthy plants, etc)?"

When we focus on the negative circumstances in our lives, how hard life is, for instance, or obsess over how wrong or unhappy we are, or worry about how little money, time, or energy we have, we empower (or fertilize) these very circumstances! Why? Because by attending to our problems we reinforce them. Inevitably such attention makes the problems more severe and we experience greater pain and unhappiness. We find more to complain about.

The paradox is that we create our pain and then *resist* it. But that which we *resist*, persists. Fighting against, or *resisting* our life circumstances or our own thoughts, for that matter, does not eliminate the limiting beliefs behind them. Rather it solidifies them or makes them stronger. If we truly want to cease being a *victim*, we must attend to, cultivate, grow positive thoughts/beliefs.

As we apply these basic principles to our lives, we begin to interact with others differently. Instead of being entrapped in the old, familiar roles of *rescuer, persecutor, victim*, we are able to respond from the much *higher frequencies* of *nurturer, asserter, and observer.* We are able to respond in ways that transpose the *victim triangle*! In so doing we literally transform the *victim triangle* into a *triangle of health and well-being.*

CHAPTER EIGHT

# The Victim Triangle Transposed

### *The Triangle of Health and Well-being*

As we experience increasing freedom from the *victim triangle*, we replace the melodrama we once thrived on with an increasing ability to *witness* or *observe* our lives. Instead of focusing on negative thoughts/beliefs that zap our energy and leave us preoccupied, resentful, and anxious, we quiet our minds and are free to *observe* and participate in the bountiful adventure that real life is.

As we grow in awareness, we are increasingly able to view *resistance* as an opportunity for growth rather than as a problem. Instead of resorting to old behaviors that would have us deny, blame, or *defend* uncomfortable feelings/beliefs/stories, we take responsibility for the situations we face and we transform those situations by effectively applying certain principles and tools.

In other words, through practice we no longer *react* automatically from a *victim mentality*; instead we are able to process our negative thoughts rather than blindly *react*. We turn the *victim triangle*, which we used previously to verify our painful beliefs/stories, on its head - right side up. Indeed we not only transpose the triangle, we transform it into a *triangle of health and well-being*.

### The *Observer*: The *Victim* Transformed

The newly transposed *triangle* sits on its base (see diagram, p. 46). At its apex is the *observer*, the *victim* transformed. When we stop blaming our unhappiness/happiness on what is happening outside of us and start *observing/witnessing* life instead, we have tapped into our *observer consciousness*. We become *observers*, rather than *victims*. We *observe* with keen interest what happens

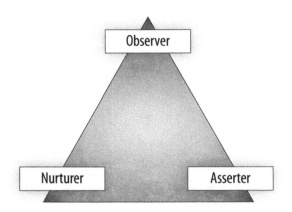

in our lives because we know there are no coincidences, no accidents. As *observers* we see everything that happens as supporting our journey towards greater consciousness. In other words, we view the world as a mirror that reflects to us our present level of consciousness.

Pure *observer consciousness* does not judge; it watches with open curiosity. It does not operate from unconscious "shoulds" and "shouldn'ts." It does not *defend* itself, nor does it assign blame. It simply *witnesses* and gathers data. *Observer consciousness* is always in present time; it is based in the *NOW*, rather than being dominated by past memories or anticipated future events. When we are in *observer consciousness*, we see life objectively and with loving detachment. We no longer see it through eyes that find imperfection and misfortune.

*Observer consciousness* vibrates at a *high-frequency*, exuding an obvious "scent of peace." Free of negative thoughts/beliefs/stories, *observer consciousness* sees life clearly and is able to respond appropriately to external stimuli. Rather than fearing the outside world, and in turn, blaming it for our problems, those in the state of *observer consciousness* become compassionate *witnesses* to circumstances. This new *observer consciousness* sits at the top of the *triangle of health and well-being*. It is who we are and it guides through intuition. It is our best self.

*Guiding Principles for Life*

Once *observer consciousness* is activated, we are then able to transform both the *persecutor* and *rescuer* roles on the *victim triangle*. We bring those *low-frequency* roles out of the dark shadows so that we may shine the light of consciousness on them and use them constructively to advance our health and well-being.

### *Asserter*: The *Persecutor* Transformed

When, as *starting gate persecutors*, we modify our aggressiveness with self-acceptance, we become diplomatic and assertive. As *asserters*, we are not afraid to tell the truth. We are confident. We are grounded in *Reality* and yet are willing to take risks to grow. As *asserters*, we comfortably stand in the truth. The truth, or *Reality*, enables us to see and speak to those around us with more clarity, more respect, more love. Where once, as *persecutors*, we perceived life as dangerous, now, as *asserters*, we perceive it as positively abundant.

We recognize quickly when old defense mechanisms arise, and, just as quickly, instead of looking around for someone or something to blame, we adjust our thoughts/beliefs. We are able then to respond with the calm, clear, and loving firmness that surfaces naturally when we expect peace and *sanity* to prevail.

We learn to see the world as a reflection of our own mind. We no longer see it as objectively cruel. We know that we are not its *victims* and so we stop automatically lashing out at others. We no longer take such quick offense at what's happening around us, nor do we feel the constant need to *defend* ourselves from some perceived attack. Instead, we respond to life from a place of conscious intention, self-control, appropriate concern, and peace.

As *asserters*, we have *boundaries* and we know them. We also recognize and honor other people's *boundaries*. We no longer feel territorial; instead, we radiate self-assurance. As a result, there is an air about us that prompts others to treat us with respect and ease.

*Asserters* are problem-solvers who know how to act decisively, efficiently, and with speed. Others find it easy to be around us because we stop insisting on being right. Because mistakes are no longer threatening to us, we can risk admitting when we're wrong.

We no longer search for proof that others are trying to take advantage of us. We cease being paranoid because we have let go of the constant anxiety and fear that characterizes *persecutors*. No longer *victims*, we begin to celebrate our freedom by pursuing our dreams. We understand that there is no one, short of ourselves, who can stop us from enjoying our lives.

### *Nurturer*: The *Rescuer* Transformed

Transformation is possible even for those of us who have been consummate *starting gate rescuers* on the *victim triangle*. Once we focus on taking care of ourselves, our priorities shift and we become true *nurturers*. Instead of *rescuing* others, we befriend ourselves first and only then do we extend a hand to others.

We empower others rather than enable them to become more dependent on us. Because our former experiences as *rescuers* made us aware of others' suffering, albeit in a skewed manner, we can more quickly become compassionate, receptive, authentic, and wise in our relations with loved ones, even as we establish necessary *boundaries*. We affirm to ourselves that others are able to be responsible for themselves.

Because we give ourselves the approval we previously sought from others, we no longer rely only on others for our sense of worth. We no longer feel compelled to compromise our values/principles to get from others that validation of self-worth. We replace the habitual pandering and care-taking we once practiced with appropriate, positive, and life-affirming interaction.

Being a *nurturer*, we know that the most loving thing we can do for loved ones is to respect their ability to pursue their own goals whether or not we understand or approve of their choices. Rather than seeing them as weaklings that need to be fixed, we adjust our thoughts/beliefs/actions so that we allow ourselves to allow others to experience and learn from the consequences of their own choices and mistakes. We are no longer tempted then to take responsibility for their problems or the outcomes in their lives. In other words, we understand more clearly what is our business and what is not. Both as *asserters*, and now as *nurturers*, we develop clear *boundaries*.

Because we have learned to look within to *Source* for the love and acceptance we once sought through care-taking, we, as *nurturers*, develop an intuitive sense of when and how to offer appropriate support. We become available to truly serve others. We no longer have an agenda to be anyone's savior. We act, instead, from a place of deep integrity and inner guidance, doing only what is best for everyone involved.

Recovery from the role of *rescuer* means that we get honest with ourselves. We begin to sort through our past agendas, motives, and limiting beliefs, and we forgive ourselves. We learn to ponder and investigate those agendas, motives, and limiting beliefs, and we see more and more clearly how they kept us stuck for so long in the *rescuer* role and on the *victim triangle*. As a result, we come to truly value the experience of making our emotional process conscious.

We learn how to investigate our beliefs and feelings, how to come to greater self-awareness, and how to open to whole new possibilities. A healthy sense of detachment develops as we deepen our trust in whatever happens.

## *Summary*

In the first half of this book we explored the nature of the *victim consciousness*: how it originates and the part *victim consciousness* plays in creating and verifying *core beliefs*. We further explored the three roles on the *victim triangle: rescuer, persecutor, victim*. We described  the *triangle of health and well-being* (the transformed *victim triangle*) and its *higher frequency* roles of *observer, asserter*, and *nurturer*.

The next part of this book outlines the practical steps we must take to transform our *victim consciousness* into a consciousness of health, peace and well-being.

# PART II

## Transforming Victim Consciousness

CHAPTER ONE

# Where to Begin our Process

We have been learning that what we think/believe, and consequently our state of mind, is our responsibility alone. If
we want to be happy and to enjoy well-being we must be willing to
accept one hundred percent responsibility for ourselves. We must
learn to look within our own minds for the support, peace, and
acceptance we previously sought in outside circumstances.

There are certain practices and techniques that can help us to
accept full responsibility for our lives and pave the way for healthier relationships with ourselves and the world. Part II of this book
presents those practices and techniques. We will study an actual
step-by-step process that will help us to transform how we think.
That transformation will liberate us from *victim consciousness.*

## Following Simple Directives

There are three simple directives that will deliver us from the *victim consciousness* that holds us captive to limiting beliefs. These
three directives are: *show up* (be present and willing), *align* (with
a *higher frequency*) and *clear* (negative beliefs). By remembering these directives and by reminding ourselves to practice them
everyday, we can *align* with *Reality/Source, clear* ourselves of negative thoughts/beliefs, and replace our *victim consciousness* with
inner peace and calm.

### Show Up

To *show up* is the first requirement for "waking up." When we
*show up*, we send a signal, to ourselves and to *Source*, that we are
ready and willing to examine our present state and look directly

at what is. In other words, we become fully present in the here and now. We are able then to consciously, deliberately, and freely examine our state of mind in the present moment. We become "awake" *observers* rather than half-asleep *reactors*.

As awake *observers* we are in a state of what I call *observer consciousness* that allows us to see every life experience as a learning opportunity for consciousness. As *observers*, rather than *reactors*, we see the challenges of our daily lives as opportunities. Consequently, lessons learned through our daily experiences offer us greater clarity and refine our consciousness. We are nudged, sometimes even shoved, into expanding our sense of who we are. Our daily life lessons shape and refine our conscious mind. To *show up* is to allow us to identify and intervene immediately when life-limiting patterns try to keep us stuck in *victim consciousness*.

### Align

The boldest act we can take towards self-responsibility is to commit to the *daily practice* with the intention to *align* with *Source*. Even when we feel good, and especially those times when we think we don't need to practice, we commit to start each day by *aligning* with *Source*. By *aligning* with such *high-frequency* thought/energy we come into active, living relationship with *Source*. To mentally, emotionally, and physically *align* with the *higher frequency* of *Source* is the second requirement in the process of waking up.

To *align* is to choose to give our full attention to some sort of centering practice with the intention of experiencing ourselves in harmony with *Source*. To *align* our personal will with the will of *Source* is the goal, so that we can be of service to *Source*. We start by cultivating a relationship with *Reality*.

Although we can cultivate a relationship with *Source* by reading or studying spiritual textbooks, there is nothing more potent or life transforming than the experience gained from having a personal daily relationship with *Source*. Spiritual textbooks like, The Kybalion (The Three Initiates, 1912) provide knowledge about the laws that govern our relationship with the Universe. But to *align* with *Source* by committing to the *daily practice* brings us into a state of familiarity and comfort with *Source* that enhances our relationship with it. In the same way that all of our relationships need time and attention to flourish, our relationship with *Source* must also be tended. The *daily practice* is when we spend time with *Source*. Through daily dialog with *Source* we are supported, healed, and guided.

Although we practice *aligning* with *Source* in our *daily practice, alignment* is not something we restrict to practicing only once a day. We come to rely on the practice of *aligning* throughout our day. We turn to it whenever we feel anxiety or *resistance* of any kind; when we are confused or can't figure something out, when we don't know the answer, when we are in the midst of a life problem, we stop a moment and set our intention to *align*. We humbly acknowledge our limited personal power and seek instead to *align* with a power that is infinitely greater. By taking a few deep breaths and turning within, we look for guidance. Such efforts bring immediate relief and guidance. The results are often profound. *Alignment* practiced regularly alleviates depression, fear, and loneliness, We no longer feel alone in facing life; we are linked with an infallible source of support that is ever present and available to us.

When we *align*, then, we choose to recognize the authority of *Source* and trust that it has purpose, intention, and benevolence. We cannot relax into *Reality* fully until we can let go of the idea that life is out to "get us." We replace that sort of nihilistic thinking with a willingness to focus on a *Source* who shows us through *Reality* the physical manifestation of our beliefs in action. We must learn how to differentiate between our *personal reality*, a limited version of *Reality* based on our own distorted perceptions/ *core beliefs*, and the true *Reality* of *Source*.

One example of distorted *personal reality* is the widely shared perception that *Source* is the cause of what we perceive to be the terrible, bad happenings in our world. How can we expect ourselves to surrender into the arms of a *Source* we believe capable of the kind of madness we perceive going on around us? Trust is imperative for change to take place and if we are to trust *Source* we must believe that it is benevolent, loving, and kind. Otherwise we cannot surrender into trusting it. *Sanity* prevails when we realize that what we perceive in the world is our own *projected* beliefs. This means that as we *clear* the limited perceptions of our *personal reality*, we come into a greater experience of the peace and grace that accompanies *Source Reality*.

Our *personal reality* is a reflection of our beliefs in action, which means that what we believe is what we will perceive as *reality*. These beliefs-in-action often create false realities, which are very different from the *Reality* of *Source*. Everything we perceive does have a cause. The cause however is not the external events or circumstances of our lives, nor is "God's will" necessarily the cause. The cause behind what we see and experience in life is our own personal (and collective) *core beliefs*. What we see in life is caused by what we as individuals, as a culture, and as a race, at core, believe. In other words, we believe our thoughts into *reality*. *Source* allows us the free will to believe whatever we choose, but we must come to understand that the price we pay (and the harvest we reap) for that freedom is the inevitable *projection* and manifestation of those beliefs into physical *reality* where we will experience them in concrete form. *Source,* the dispassionate *observer,* simply sees and accepts the world we create with our thoughts/beliefs. Without judgment or ridicule, *Source* steadily shines the light of consciousness so that we may see more clearly the *core beliefs* we hold that determine our life experience.

### Clear

To *clear* is the third prerequisite for awakening from *victim consciousness.* The rest of this book will explore these three directives: to *show up, align* and *clear.* We will learn techniques designed to help us raise our *vibrational frequency* by identifying our negative *core beliefs*, and techniques to *clear* our negative mental chatter. We will learn to question our painful thoughts/beliefs/stories using The Work of Byron Katie (www.thework.com). Finally, we will learn, through a body-centered practice, how to apply these methods to *clear* the physical body of stress and pain.

We will add methods for *clearing* to our *daily practice*. We see *clearing* as an essential part of our *alignment* with *Source*. Making a commitment to *clear* is the action part of recovery from *victim consciousness*. How we answer the following questions is an indicator of our level of willingness in making such a commitment: "How badly do I want to be free of *victim consciousness*? "Am I serious enough to make a daily commitment to *align* with *Source*? How committed am I to a *daily practice* towards achieving inner peace?"

If these questions inspire in us a great longing for freedom and peace, then that is good. Let that longing motivate us to apply the methods described herein to free us from *victim consciousness*. We begin by paying close attention to whenever we feel bad; we recognize such feelings as helpful signals to identify negative thoughts/beliefs/stories we need to *clear*.

When used consistently, the three directives, *show up, align,* and *clear*, help us stay sane in a world that otherwise confounds us with its chaos. Learning to practice them grounds us in a *Reality* that is joyously rewarding. We will begin to experience life in a radically different way. The more we *clear*, the better we are able to relax and trust that the universe is bringing us exactly what we need. No longer feeling the need to protect ourselves from what we once perceived as threatening circumstances/people/events, we experience less *resistance* towards life situations. We no longer view external *Reality* as the enemy. Instead, we look inside us and choose thoughts/beliefs/actions that bring us peace and well-being.

There is a three step process that helps us apply to our daily lives in a practical way the *show-up, align,* and *clear* directives. Let's explore that process next.

## *Applying a Three Part Process for Healing*
There are three parts to the process of getting off of the *victim triangle*, away from *victim consciousness*, and into *observer consciousness*.

The three parts are as follows:

1. Cultivate a *daily practice*
2. Assume self-responsibility
3. Identify and clear *core beliefs*

We can word and prioritize these directives in various ways, for example as follows:

1. Take responsibility
2. Find underlying beliefs
3. Do something everyday

I want here to assign priority to cultivating a *daily practice* because, in my opinion, that step detemines whether or not we successfully persevere on the journey to health and overall well-being.

CHAPTER TWO

# Step 1: The Daily Practice

## *Cultivating the Daily Practice*

I define the *daily practice* as setting our *intention* on *aligning* our-selves with *Source*, and then giving that *aligning* our total atten-tion for a few minutes everyday through an action (or actions) that connects us mentally, physically, and spiritually. The *daily practice* is an activity we consciously perform at a certain time everyday for the specific purpose of *aligning* ourselves with *Source*.

That activity can be any form of meditation or movement that is designed to help us *align* our *intention* with a *higher frequency*, with *Source*.  Before we get into further detail about the nature of the *daily practice*, I want to share a story told by Jeanne Yves Leloup (2003), a French researcher who writes about early Christi-anity. This story is found in his book, <u>Being Still, Reflections on an Ancient Mystical Tradition</u> (translated by M.S, Laird, p. 2 - 12) and recounts a philosophy student's encounter with a humble, hermit monk, Father Seraphim. The story (paraphrased here) beautifully illustrates what having a *daily practice* can do. It is a story I use often to teach the process of *alignment*. In a workbook sequel to the present book I will share a meditation based on this story; the meditation is crafted to help you find *alignment* through your own *daily practice*. But first here, as I recall it, is the story about a young man's meeting with Father Seraphim.

### Lessons from Father Seraphim

A young philosopher went to Fr. Seraphim seeking peace and enlightenment. He asked the monk to show him how to pray from his heart. After some debate, Fr. Seraphim showed him an enormous rock and said, "Before I teach you about prayer of the heart, you must learn to meditate like this mountain. Sit with it and discover how it prays. Once you've learned that, we'll talk."

The young philosopher meditated on the rock until, slowly, he began to *align* with it. He became one with the stillness and stability of the mountain, "silent under the sun." (Leloup, 2003: p.3), And then one day, several months later, Fr. Seraphim came and abruptly demanded that the young man stop meditating on the mountain.

He led his student instead to a poppy flower growing among the herbs in his wildflower garden and told him to sit with the poppy as he had with the mountain, and to meditate on the flower, but without giving up what he had learned from the mountain. The young man sat many days with the poppy flower until he was able to merge with it. His meditation on the poppy taught him how to seek *alignment* with *Source* the way the poppy sought constant *alignment* with its source, the sun.

Soon thereafter Fr. Seraphim walked down from the mountain with the student and led him to the ocean shore. There he sat him down in front of the ocean and told the avid student to meditate on the ocean, retaining what he had learned from his previous meditations with the mountain and the poppy. This time he urged the young man to use his breath to become one with the waves while meditating on the ocean.

The young philosopher's meditation was deepened as he sat silent, grounded like a mountain, his spine straight and supple like the tall, lithe stem of a poppy flower seeking to *align* with the sun, while he breathed in rhythm and harmony with the ocean. The *physical alignment* the young man gained through his meditations made possible Fr. Seraphim's next assignment: the student was encouraged to listen closely and meditate on the cooing of a pair of lovebirds nesting in the eves of an old hermit's hut nearby.

At first the young man was distracted from stillness by the constant noise of the pair of lovebirds, but then Fr. Seraphim explained how the pair were constantly praising their creator and were therefore perfect models of how to attain a singing, grateful heart. After some days of meditating on the cooing birds, the young man began to experience a wellspring of joy and praise bubbling up from his own heart that inspired spontaneous words of praise and adoration to come forth from his own lips.

Finally one day, Fr. Seraphim told the young man that he was now ready to meditate like a human being. The young philosopher had learned much about how the natural world *aligns* and communes with *Source*. Now, said Fr. Seraphim, it was time for the student to meditate upon the prophet, Abraham.

Fr. Seraphim reminded his student about the faith of Abraham and his complete obedience to God. He encouraged the young man to retain the lessons learned from the mountain, the poppy, the ocean, and the birds as he meditated on the unquestioned obedience of Abraham who had been willing to surrender all that he was, all that he had, to God, even his own son.

It took awhile for the young man to merge into the surrender and faith of Abraham; at times the monk would come upon the young man absorbed in his meditation, his face wet with tears of compassion and surrender. Finally he was ready to seek further instruction. He asked Fr. Seraphim why he had not talked with him about Christ. The monk became immediately pensive and quiet. He said, "Only Christ can teach you about Christ. You must bring all the wisdom you have gained from your meditation into your meeting and merger with the Christ." I have shared with you all the steps to create heart prayer; this last step is one that will bring you into oneness with Christ." The young man spent some time there on the mountain finding oneness with Christ. Sometimes he would be so absorbed in the merger that his own separate identity was forgotten. After some time of such open-hearted meditation, Fr. Seraphim sent him away. The young philosopher returned to his home where he continued to integrate his mountain meditation experience into his most ordinary, day-to-day, life (Leloup, 2003).

I tell a condensed version of this beautiful story here to illustrate the essential ingredients in a *process of alignment*: grounded stability, physical *alignment*, rhythmic breath, a rejoicing heart, complete surrender, and total merger with *Source*. This meditation *aligns* the whole being: our physical body (focusing on the mountain, poppy and ocean), our emotional self (focusing on the joy of the singing birds), and our mental, spiritual selves (meditating on Abraham's obedience and surrender), leading to the ultimate spiritual merger with *Source* (Christ). Such at-one-ment with *Source* is the complete antithesis of *victim consciousness*. Finding *alignment* with *Source* is the goal and the purpose of the *daily practice*. Now that we've established what the *daily practice* can do, let's talk in more detail about what it is and why it's important.

If we are serious about the first directive, to *show up*, then we must begin to practice it daily. Through the *daily practice*, we develop the habit of turning away from mental noise and unhappy images to what is real, to *Reality*.

*Reality*, remember, does not consist of our opinions, fears, beliefs or thoughts; *Reality* consists of the bare bone facts. It can be demonstrated through the senses; *Reality* consists of what we see, hear, touch, taste and smell. It simply is what is.

However, there is a component of *Reality* that is not so readily perceivable through the senses. We experience this Unseen *Reality* through certain unchanging principles that govern life. Such principles are universal laws that govern all manifestation. The most essential, basic law is this one: there is only one Mind; everything is a part of that One Mind. Duality/separation is an illusion. The One Mind has been called by many names, including God, Yahweh, Great Spirit, etc; I call the One Mind/*Reality* by the name *Source* because it is indeed the one true *Source* from which all things come.

Although we will learn about other universal principles, the basic fundamental truth stated simply as, "All is One," is the foundation for everything presented here. Our task in this book is to show the difference between the thoughts and beliefs we mistake for *Reality* and *Reality* itself. The ultimate cause of our unhappiness in life is this mistake; we are confused about what is and what is not *Reality*.

What we think and feel is our *reaction to Reality*, and not *Reality* itself. What we think and feel comes from what we believe.

What we believe is not *Reality*, but a story about *Reality*. These thoughts/beliefs that we have about what we see/hear/etc may, or may not, be true. The tool we cultivate to help us make the distinction between our unhappy beliefs about *Reality* and *Reality* itself is the *daily practice*. It furthers us in our ability to separate illusion from fact and helps us make the necessary *frequency adjustment* towards *aligning* with what is real.

One of the most painful costs of living on the *victim triangle* is that we lose our sense of *Reality*. When we identify with our limited, negative thoughts/stories/beliefs, we lose touch with *Reality*, and with who we really are. When we experience this loss we often desperately look for some external person or thing that will "fix" what is missing in us instead of turning inward to where *Reality* can be found. What we don't realize is that by looking to the outside world for our answers, we are abandoning *Reality*; in short we abandon ourselves! No wonder we feel so internally lost. Our first task then, on the journey to well-being, is to consciously reconnect with *Reality*, with the inborn, essential self with whom we have lost touch. Otherwise we cannot escape *victim consciousness*.

The *daily practice* helps us remember who we are beyond our physical constraints and limitations. We are not the limited beliefs we have adopted. We are more than mere bodies and brains in motion; we are more than our biases and fears. We are larger and more expanded than anything physical bodies or limiting beliefs can contain. We are part of the Universal Mind/*Source*, and we must remember that to truly free ourselves. The most powerful and essential step we can take towards remembering who we are is to develop and commit to the *daily practice*. The *daily practice* serves to anchor us in *Reality* and move us firmly towards health and well-being.

## Nourishing Our Three Bodies through Daily Practice
To move into *alignment* with *Reality* and accomplish a state of well-being and health, we must meet the needs of our mental, emotional and physical body. These three bodies comprise the sum total of our personal self. Each of these bodies must be

brought into *alignment* in its own unique way to fully accomplish mental and emotional freedom from *victim consciousness*.

There are many ways of bringing each of these bodies into *alignment*. Many disciplines address the needs of only one or two bodies and neglect the third. For instance there is much instruction available in the world on ways to address and restructure problematic thinking, as well as ways to bring about emotional *clearing* and address physical concerns. But the importance of addressing the whole personal self - mind, emotions and the physical body - are not often highlighted.

I have heard it said that healing happens first on the mind level. We become aware that the way we think is confused. As we begin to look at the way we think, we come to realize that our emotional self is a product of the way we think (what we believe) and must be examined. Our feelings must be brought into *alignment* with *Reality*. Last, but far from least, we must address the concerns of our physical body to complete a full *alignment* of our *personal reality* with *Source*. The *daily practice* is a discipline that *aligns* and connects us with *Source* energy on all levels, physical mental/spiritual, and emotional.

A good *daily practice* will include ways for the three bodies of our personal self to *show-up, align,* and *clear*. It is advisable to sample several suggestions for a *daily practice* until we find activities/movements, or a combination thereof that most effectively meet the needs of the whole self.

As important as it is for us to commit to a *daily practice*, it is even more essential to nourish our personal self by cultivating the right attitude towards doing the practice. To establish the right attitude, we simply set our *intention* to consciously focus on the *highest frequency* possible which is, of course, *Source*. And the best way to *align* with *Source* is to dedicate our whole practice, every day, to the sole purpose of connecting our whole selves with *Source*.

Through the *daily practice*, we might use yoga, *qigong*, or tai chi as a type of body prayer that stretches and conditions the physical body so it not only functions at its best, but allows it to become a physical temple through which we can experience the presence of *Source*.

Through increasing body awareness we heighten our overall consciousness. In the same way that a desk lamp must be plugged in to an electrical outlet to work properly, we must be similarly plugged in to *Source* energy. We use our physical body to plug ourselves into, or connect with, *Source*.

The main function of practices like yoga and *qigong* is to learn the right physical *alignment* for best handling the *high-frequency* energy that flows into and through us when we are consciously connected with *Source*. The better we are at finding the appropriate process for *aligning* ourselves physically, the more universal energy we can contain. This universal flow of *Source* energy in and through us enables us to rejuvenate and heal our bodies and minds. In that way we actually become an embodiment of *Source* energy.

Such physical *alignment* can also be facilitated through music and song, chanting, poetry, and/or breathing meditations, to further open our hearts and thus *align* our emotional body with *Source*. We begin, as well, to learn ways to *clear* painful emotion through the *daily practice*. To feed the mind and *align* our thinking to bring the mental body into *alignment*, we can read, journal, or meditate on a symbol or verse. By reaching to *Source* through meditative practices we strengthen our whole body and receive deep healing benefits. The personal body can then become a finely tuned instrument in service to the *highest frequency possible - Source*.

The *daily practice* is much more than just a regular exercise or meditation routine; it is an intimate conversation and connection with *Source*. It is a dialog, or ongoing exchange, between us and the Universal Living Intelligence. Such a practice truly can transform us.

We use the *daily practice*, not just to stay fit or to say we have a practice but to reach for the *highest frequency* possible. We do it so we can transform our *victim consciousness* to a consciousness that goes beyond the physical: an *observer consciousness* which releases us completely from *victim consciousness*.

## Finding Right Attitude through Daily Practice

Rather than being motivated from a place of conformity, through the *daily practice* we are motivated to achieve more than anything else a state of inner freedom and connection with *Source*. When we maintain a sincere and relentless longing to know our true selves and *Source*, we fuel our commitment to that *daily practice*.

Out of this longing for, and commitment to, union with *Source* come the two essential ingredients for maintaining a right attitude: *intention* and *sincerity*. It is those two qualities that determine the effectiveness of our practice, rather than any particular activity/movement. An effective practice, in turn, leads us to *surrender* deeply to *Source* and opens us to receive the gifts of health and well-being we seek.

In order, then, to foster a right attitude towards the *daily practice*, we must set our *intention*. We set our *intention* to *align* with a positive goal or direction.

We start the *daily practice*, then, by *intending* a connection with *Source*. In other words, we consciously choose to focus our minds on the *highest frequency* possible by reading inspirational literature, for instance, or by praying, or by meditating on a higher thought. Establishing right *intention* is a powerful concept because it implies a conscious directing of our personal will or desire. It is powerful precisely because it directs universal energy. Practicing right *intention* restores health, rejuvenates the body, and liberates the mind.

If we practice out of habit or from a sense of duty, or because we think we should, or because we are trying to prove how spiritually evolved we are, we do not have *sincerity*. When we approach the *daily practice* with anticipation and delight, with reverence and gratitude, as if we are having a private and very intimate meeting with our most beloved friend, we put ourselves in a state of *sincerity*. Practicing with *sincerity* deepens the authenticity of the *daily practice*. My *qigong* teacher, Jeff Primack of <u>Supreme Science</u>

Qigong Foundation (S.S.Q.F.)(http://qigong.com/), says that when we practice with *sincerity*, the benefits increase one-hundredfold over an average, routine practice. When our *intention* and *sincerity* become firm through *daily practice*, we are able to *surrender*.

To *surrender* means to let go or trust. When we consciously and sincerely trust *Source* and *align* with *Source*, we practice *surrendering* to its promptings. Our ability to let go/trust/*surrender* grows as we continue our practice, because *surrendering* happens naturally when we habitually trust *Source* as our friend and benefactor. An attitude of *surrender* is essential to having an effective *daily practice*.

Through the *daily practice*, both characteristics of right attitude (*intention* and *sincerity*), and the *surrender* they lead to, become stronger and deeper. Imagine then the power and healing potential of a conscious, sincere *daily practice*!

## Recognizing the Benefits of Daily Practice

The benefits of having a conscious, sincere, and trusting *daily practice* are both immediate and immense. The *daily practice* benefits our being (who we are) and our actions (how we behave).

**Benefits for our Being *(who we are)*:**
1. We *observe* more clearly what's happening around us.
2. We become more grounded and experience a better connection to ourselves and others.
3. We grow in well-being and security because we know that we are in direct contact with *Source* and that we are protected and cared for.
4. We feel less alone, more at home in ourselves, and with those around us.
5. We no longer define ourselves by limiting, negative concepts/beliefs.

**Benefits for our Actions (*how we behave*):**
6. We are able to take risks to grow emotionally and spiritually because we trust *Source*.

7. We can initiate positive change.
8. We are better able to deal with everyday issues. Challenges we might have once considered to be insurmountable become, instead, steps for refining consciousness.
9. We respond to life with wisdom and compassion, rather than *reacting*, as we once did, from a state of high stress and frustration.
10. We express in our lives the alive, intelligent Universal *Source* that responds to all of our needs and desires.

As we experience these, and similar results/benefits, we find it difficult to imagine ever returning to a life that does not include some kind of *daily practice*.

## Cultivating Observer Consciousness through Daily Practice

The *daily practice* is the most powerful way to cultivate our *observer consciousness*. The *observer consciousness* is an integral agent in the recovery process, and it can be activated and strengthened in many ways: through books on self-discovery and spirituality, therapy, body-work, etc. It is through our *daily practice,* however, that we become truly proficient at accessing and living in o*bserver consciousness*.

The *observer consciousness* is essential if we are to be free from *victim consciousness*. The ability to *observe* our thoughts/beliefs makes transformation possible. *Observing* the circumstances of our lives with dispassion and acceptance develops as a result of the *daily practice*!

We must be able to *observe* ourselves without judgment if we are going to really progress. Negative judgments distort our ability to clearly *observe* ourselves because whatever we judge as unacceptable, we automatically deny and suppress. *Observing* truth/ *Reality* then is impossible when we judge/deny/suppress *Reality*! On the other hand, when we tap into our *observer consciousness* we no longer deny/suppress our negative thoughts and feelings. Instead, we cultivate an accepting and forgiving attitude which allows us to let go of negative thoughts/feelings.

Developing a clear, strong *observer consciousness* is the biggest reward the *daily practice* offers and it is the gift out of which all other benefits are born. As a matter of fact, the *observer consciousness* can be said to be the source of all the benefits we listed above, benefits such as, rising above life challenges, and increased confidence and trust in *Source*. The latter are actually characteristics of *observer consciousness*. It is our *observer consciousness* which recognizes when we are on the *victim triangle*, which questions our thoughts/beliefs, and which reports to us whether we are in a *high* or a *low-frequency*.

The higher *frequency* of *observer consciousness* grounds us in truth/*Reality*, returns us to *sanity*, and ultimately, transforms us. Strengthening *observer consciousness* through practice is the single most effective step we can take towards freeing our minds from *victim consciousness*. The *observer* is who we are when we truly *show up*.

We greatly enhance our own personal process of transformation by setting aside time every day to experience *Source* energy. Through the *daily practice* we cultivate *observer consciousness* which is the essential consciousness needed to move us out of *victim consciousness*. Through dispassionate seeing, *observer consciousness* links us with *Source* so that freedom from *victim consciousness* becomes possible.

Unless we are spending time in listening silence or practicing some sort of *alignment* (such as yoga/*qigong*/Tai Ji, etc), we cannot access the full healing and transformative experience that comes from personal contact with *Source*. Nothing else, no amount of reading, thinking, or seeking resolution and relief in the external world will bring us the results we seek.

Rather than looking for solutions externally, we turn inward by cultivating the *daily practice*. Using the tools of *intention* and *sincerity*, we acknowledge *Source*, and *surrender* in appreciation to *Source*. In so doing, we not only free ourselves from the *victim triangle*, we forever change the way we see ourselves and the world.

As we awaken our *observer consciousness* through a committed *daily practice* we become increasingly aware of the importance of assuming full responsibility for our lives. We do so by becoming radically honest with ourselves. Becoming radically honest and assuming self-responsibility are essential next steps on our journey to health and well-being.

# CHAPTER THREE

# Step 2: Self-Responsibility

To maintain freedom from *victim consciousness* it is most important that we become completely honest with ourselves. Being completely honest means facing the truth about ourselves. Only then are we able to accept full responsibility for making the changes necessary to restore health and establish well-being.

After we have identified where we are on the *victim triangle* we must examine what that means and tell ourselves the truth about it. Otherwise we will never see, much less be able to assume responsibility for, the thinking that keeps us there. To be self-responsible is to be unashamedly and lovingly candid with ourselves so we can see, and therefore take action to address that in us which is keeping us stuck. These two, truth and self-responsibility, are tacit partners in accomplishing step two of freeing ourselves from the *victim triangle*.

When we are radically honest with ourselves and assume full responsibility for who we are and how we behave, we no longer stubbornly insist we are right. We understand and become willing to admit that our thoughts, not outside circumstances, cause our unhappiness. We stop blaming others for our feelings. In short, we learn to take one hundred percent responsibility for who we are and how we behave. Such self-awareness allows us to quickly shift our feelings, thoughts, and behavior to a more productive state of being and action.

Because we know it is what we tell ourselves about a situation that causes our happiness/unhappiness, we can assume responsibility for our own happiness/unhappiness. We are open, more willing even, to seeing the thoughts generated in *victim consciousness* for what they are: obstacles to peace. Not surprisingly, we then become unflinching in our resolve to find what thoughts/beliefs are causing us distress, so that we can more quickly resolve them.

It is important to remember, however, that there is no place for negative self-judgment in the process of assuming self-responsibility. Negative self-judgment only hinders our ability to assume it. It keeps us feeling bad about ourselves, and as a result, we continue to deny that we are still in *victim consciousness*.

Most of us grew up believing that taking care of ourselves before we take care of others is selfish and indeed wrong. Taking care of ourselves first, however, is not being selfish. It is really the only way to move off of the *victim triangle* and out of *victim consciousness*. It is the most effective way to be available to others. When we neglect ourselves, physically and emotionally, we foster eventual and long term dependency on others. We, in effect, assume the role of a *victim* and demand that someone else *rescue* us (spouses, children, other family and friends). When we recognize this fact, we see that it is not only essential, it is also unselfish, to put ourselves first!

I am reminded of a time when a client said to me, "It just seems, Lynne, that you do take care of yourself before taking care of anyone else." I responded, "Yes, you are right. I do see my own life and taking care of myself as a priority. It is very important to me. And I have been diligently attempting to teach you to put yourself first! After all, who could possibly take better care of us than ourselves?"

Taking care of ourselves is our number one job. Only then are we free to be available in service to *Source* and others.

## Avoiding Self-Responsibility

To take care of ourselves we must begin to recognize the ways we don't assume self-responsibility. There are many ways we habitually avoid self-responsibility. I've included here some of the common and most insidious ones.

## Blaming Others

To fully take charge of ourselves means we must let go of the compulsion to blame people and situations outside of ourselves for our unhappiness. But doing that can be difficult for those of us who grew up believing that the external world determines our feelings. It becomes easier to see the fallacy in this way of thinking as we *observe* the many varieties of *reaction* that a single event can evoke.

For instance, let's say that two friends come to visit. When they arrive they find us in the garden weeding. Instead of inviting them in, we opt to serve tea there in the garden. Later, we learn that our garden visitors had very different stories about the quality of our afternoon together.

One of our visitors was indeed delighted that we had opted for tea in the garden among the flowers and fresh air. However our second visitor was not quite so content. As a matter of fact, she was quite upset, feeling offended and resentful because she felt we slighted her by serving her tea outside in the garden, rather than inviting her into the house. Her unhappy story had her believing that we did not value her enough to invite her inside our home. To her way of thinking, serving tea in the garden was evidence that we thought of her as less important than those we might have served in the house.

So, one of our visitors felt complimented and delighted to be served tea in the garden; the other felt hurt and resentful about it. Why the different responses? Obviously it was not the situation that determined their very different feelings. What they each told themselves about the situation within their own minds determined each one's *reaction*!

Anytime we see an outside situation, person or event as being the cause of our unhappiness, we are in v*ictim consciousness* because we are blaming outside events, rather than assuming self-responsibility. We are seeing ourselves as being at the mercy of something outside of ourselves, and that leaves us feeling helpless and resentful. Again, we are the ones who are responsible for what we feel, not another person or some external situation. Giving up blame is a powerful way to move off of the *victim triangle* and out of *victim consciousness.*

## Denying *Reality*

Part of assuming responsibility for ourselves entails learning to differentiate between *Reality* and our perception of *Reality,* i.e. our *personal reality.* In the example presented above, for instance, we simply served tea to our visitors in the garden. How the visitors interpreted that event, what they told themselves about its meaning, etc. is their perception of *Reality,* and not *Reality* itself. We can see then how two people can *witness* the very same event and have totally different perceptions of it and therefore two totally different *reactions* to it.

Our *personal reality* determines our emotional *vibrational frequency.* Again, using the garden tea example above, we can notice that our discontented visitor's perception (that the host slighted her by serving tea in the garden rather than in the house) generated in her feelings of resentment and separation. Hers was a *low-frequency* viewpoint because she interpreted the situation in a way that lowered her emotional vibration and left her feeling bad. The other friend perceived the event in a way that created positive feelings. Her perspective, therefore, was of a *higher frequency.*

As we mentioned previously, the thoughts that generate a positive sense of connection, peace, contentment, etc. are not ones we need to concern ourselves with. It is the *low-frequency* thoughts that need our intervention. Interestingly enough, even though *low-frequency* thoughts generate much misery for us, we often insist on holding on to them; we want to be right, no matter the cost.

## Being Right

When we have the *consciousness* of a *victim,* we are addicted to being "right." When we are in any of the three roles – *victim, persecutor,* or *rescuer* – we find it difficult to admit we are wrong, even to ourselves. Instead of owning our behavior we insist that someone else is to blame for what we said or did. As long as we deny and/or justify our negative behavior we make getting off the *victim triangle* impossible.

<u>A Course In Miracles</u> (Foundation for Inner Peace, 1976) asks a pertinent and important question relevant to this discussion: "Do you prefer that you be right or happy?" When we are honest with ourselves, we acknowledge our tendency to being more interested in being right than in finding inner peace and harmony with others. We would rather prove our less-than-happy perception of *Reality* - our *personal reality* - than enjoy peace and happiness. Recovery from *victim consciousness* means reversing our priorities: we become more interested in peace and harmony than in proving we are right.

## Competing for *Victim*

The need to be right is a dynamic that often gets played out between couples as a sort of *victim competition*. I have worked with couples that have spent years of their relationship engaged in an unconscious *victim competition* with one another. Each partner was busy, in their own minds, making a case against the other about how unfairly they had been treated by their mate. Consider the following six statements, for example:

1. "You told me you were going to do something for me, but you let me down. I am always doing things for you, but you're never there for me when I need you."
2. "You blew everything I worked so hard for, and left me with nothing."
3. "You kept me from (being/doing/having) something and I suffered as a result. It's your fault."
4. "I always do everything around the house; you never help out."
5. "I often put you first, but you take me for granted."
6. "I am miserable because of the way you treat me. I would never treat you the way you treat me!"

It is easy to hear the *victim* tone in these statements. Clearly, such exchanges do not promote harmony! On the contrary, exchanges like these keep us on the *victim triangle* in a never-ending downward spiral.

We need to ask ourselves if we spend our creative energy trying to prove that our mate (or loved one) is the primary reason we are unhappy. When we spend our energy in this sort of evidence gathering, we try and try and try to make our mate treat us the way we think we should be treated, or we rant about how our mate isn't supportive, etc. If we want to free ourselves from v*ictim consciousness,* we must recognize when we are relating from a position on the *victim triangle* and acknowledge that fact not only to ourselves but to our partner as well.

## Judging Ourselves

We are more able to tell ourselves the truth once we let go of self-judgment. When we stop attacking ourselves for what we feel, do and believe, we stop *projecting* judgments onto others. We see the *Reality* (truth) of our own situation without needing an outside source to blame.

When we accept ourselves, we are honest with ourselves, making denial unnecessary. As a result, we see the truth of our situation more clearly because we feel safe enough to see it. Every time we judge ourselves harshly, we activate an automatic process of repression and *projection* that derails our progress. This repression/*projection* process operates as follows: negative self-judgment leads to denial which leads to repression which results in *projection*.

Denial and repression unfailingly follow negative self-judgment because we do not want to feel bad about ourselves. We do not want to feel guilt and self-recrimination. We find it easier to deny a certain quality in ourselves and then *project* that quality onto someone else and hate it in them. When we decide that a certain quality within us is unacceptable, it is difficult not to loathe ourselves. It is easier to look the other way and pretend that we are not like that!

When we need or want to protect and/or preserve our self-image we resort to judgment, denial, and *projection*. To become healthy, we must replace self-judgment with self-understanding. When we see ourselves, not from a place of self-disparagement, but from a place of understanding why we feel and act the way we do, we live in a way that promotes growth and well-being. Rather than judging, denying, and *projecting* undesirable feelings and behaviors, we learn from them. We find the thoughts/beliefs underlying these feelings and behaviors, admit them, and act to change them. Only by being radically honest with ourselves, will we see the thoughts/beliefs that are holding us back. It is this radical honesty that effectively facilitates change.

## Speaking Victim Vocabulary

In the first chapter of Part 1, we described *victim consciousness* as a worldwide epidemic. It's true. Everyone we know goes in and out of *victim consciousness* throughout any given day. Most of us do it without even noticing. However our language is a powerful indicator of *victim consciousness*. When we are in *victim consciousness* we speak the language that goes with it.

What we say and how we say it indicates whether we are taking responsibility for ourselves or not. Words have power. We disclose a lot about ourselves through the words we choose to use in talking about our life experiences. The words we choose expose what we really think and believe. There are distinct *victim* "catch-phrases" that actually perpetuate *victim consciousness*. I call these words and phrases *victim vocabulary* which may be defined as words or phrases that are used to blame (or credit) something outside ourselves as the cause of our state of well-being. *Victim vocabulary* communicates the belief that we (and others) are at the mercy of life.

When we learn to recognize these words or phrases that we habitually use everyday to disempower ourselves, we become increasingly aware of when we are in *victim consciousness*. Being on the lookout for such *victim* language allows us to move into our *observer consciousness* more quickly. By listening to the way we talk about ourselves and others, we become quickly skilled at spotting *victim consciousness* in ourselves and others.

The use of *victim vocabulary* reflects to us not only when we (and others) are on the *victim triangle*, but exactly where on the *victim triangle* we (and they) are at any given time. That's because each of the three primary roles on the *victim triangle*, (*rescuer, persecutor,* and *victim*) have their own particular style of speaking that serves to reinforce their position on the *victim triangle*.

I have provided a few examples below of some of the more common examples of *victim vocabulary* starting with the number one most commonly used *victim* phrase: These three words("it made me") are used unthinkingly by most of us all the time, regardless of who we are or where we are on the *victim triangle*. The phrase is most associated, however, with the *persecutor* role.

The phrase, "It (you, he, she, they) made me (feel bad, screw up, fall, etc.)" blames others. Notice the lack of self-responsibility? This example of *victim vocabulary,* when used, implies that we are at the mercy of some outside person, event or circumstance. It is pure *victim* speech, because the truth is there is only one person who can make us feel or act in any certain way and that one person is ourselves. We are the ones who make us feel, think and act the way we do.

We take full responsibility for ourselves when we exchange those two words "made (make) me" with phrases like, "I choose (to do, think, or feel), I do, I will, or I won't." Instead of using *victim* statements like, "She made me get it wrong," we learn to use more self-responsible phrases such as, "I got it wrong," or "I made a mistake." Notice the absence of blame here. We simply state the obvious. We report *Reality* instead of looking for something to blame. The use of *victim vocabulary* places blame somewhere else and in that way perpetuates *victim consciousness*. Replacing *victim vocabulary* with such options as those mentioned above allows us to assume responsibility for the outcomes in our lives and thus empowers us to act towards our own highest and best good.

Below are some other more common examples of *victim vocabulary*:

"It's not my fault."

"I couldn't help it."

"I had no choice."

"I had to do (say) it."

"I was forced to do (say) it."

Notice the sense of powerlessness that is conveyed in the above phrases. *Victim vocabulary* leaves us feeling impotent and at the mercy of our life circumstances. On the other hand, when we see a world of cause and effect we communicate very differently. Instead of speaking as *victims*, we see what we experience as an effect of our own beliefs; we see our thinking as the true cause of our life experience. Instead of saying things like, "it's not my fault," we learn to look for where our responsibility lies in every situation, not so we can blame ourselves (or others) but so we can empower ourselves! Taking responsibility, instead of blaming others, for the less desirable outcomes in our lives, frees us to take action towards achieving higher possibilities.

Even *rescuers* on the *victim triangle* speak their own brand of *victim vocabulary*. Their use of words tends to reflect their belief that they (rather than the individuals they are rescuing) are in charge of the lives and happiness of others. Through their choice of words, *rescuers* assume responsibility for everyone, but themselves. Some examples of the *victim vocabulary* of *rescuers* might be as follows:

"They are too (sick/weak/dumb/irresponsible/incapable) to take care of themselves, I must do it for them."

"I can't stand for them to suffer. I must fix it for them."

"I have to do it all. I am the only one who can."

"I sacrifice all for them because they are more important than me."

As we move out of the *rescuer* role we choose healthier ways of speaking such as the following:

"I trust them to be able to take responsibility for themselves."

"How can I support them towards assuming self-responsibility?"

"I trust that they will grow from their life challenges and have no wish to  deprive them of that
opportunity."

"I know that by letting them do their part, they will
feel more empowered and I will feel better too."

Of course there are many other examples of *victim vocabulary*
than those provided above. The main point here is to notice that
the key component of getting off the *victim triangle* is missing
in *victim vocabulary*; there is a distinct lack of self-responsibility
implied. If we want to free ourselves from *victim consciousness*, we
must begin by assuming responsibility for our thoughts, feelings
and behavior and allowing others the same right. A primary way
to assume self-responsibility is through our language. To transform our *victim consciousness*, we learn to listen for the subtle
ways we verbalize that keeps us from taking full responsibility and
exchange our use of *victim vocabulary* with ways of speaking that
communicates self-responsibility and that empowers ourselves
and others instead.

## *Developing Healthy Boundaries*

It becomes increasingly important to learn how and when to set
appropriate *boundaries* as we grow more serious about truly loving
ourselves. Setting *boundaries* is a part of taking responsibility for
ourselves. It is a fundamental part of getting off the *victim triangle*.

Setting *boundaries* is not about *reacting* in an overt, defensive
way; rather it is about responding from a clear vision of *Reality*.
Having clear *boundaries* simply means that we are very aware of
what is our business and what is not. Having good *boundaries*
means we understand that we are not responsible for the perceptions of others. We are responsible only for our own perceptions.
We stay committed to taking care of ourselves and leave others to
tend to their business.

With healthy *boundaries*, we do not become caretakers of others, nor do we need to strike out or *react* in harsh ways to protect
ourselves from some imagined persecution. Instead, we are able
to own and question the stressful beliefs that our minds create

| If I Am | If I Am Responsible for Others | If I Am Responsible to Others |
|---------|-------------------------------|-------------------------------|
| I | Manipulate<br>Fix<br>Protect<br>Rescue<br>Control<br>Demand<br>Bully<br>Carry their feelings<br>Don't Listen | Show respect<br>Trust the process<br>Show empathy<br>Encourage<br>Share<br>Honor boundaries<br>Level<br>Listen |
| I FEEL | Resentful<br>Tired<br>Anxious<br>Fearful<br>Liable<br>Guilty<br>Obligated<br>Judgemental<br>Overwhelmed | Faith<br>Congruent<br>Relaxed<br>Free<br>Aware (of reality)<br>At peace<br>Joyful<br>Unconditionally accepting |
| I WANT | Things to go my own way<br>The solution<br>External results<br>Answers<br>To control circumstances<br>To be right<br>To know all the details<br>Credit | To support reality<br>To live and let live<br>To relate person to person<br>(not to the situation)<br>To share myself:<br>To believe the other person<br>has what they need to make it.<br>To empower (not control)<br>To connect with the other |
| I AM | On the victim triangle<br>A manipulator/controller<br>A prosecutor/bully<br>An enabler<br>A caretaker/rescuer<br>A martyr/victim | Present & available<br>Self-responsible<br>Accepting of reality<br>Unconditionally supportive<br>A guide<br>A friend |

without feeling the need to *defend* or justify our acts. We know that others' behavior toward us comes from what they believe about us and that that, too, is not our business. When we own and take responsibility for our own thoughts and beliefs, we create healthy *boundaries*. We innately know what is appropriate and create accordingly.

The chart above illustrates the difference between being responsible for others (*rescuing*/care-taking) and being responsible to (empowering/supporting) others. When we take responsibility for others we send a disempowering message and our interaction with them is imbued with *victim consciousness*. We are on the *victim triangle*. When we are responsible, first and foremost, to ourselves and then to them, we send a message that empowers their belief in their own abilities and supports us in taking care of ourselves.This chart, an updated version of a handout (original author unknown) that I used in an addictions treatment center where I worked in the eighties, shows that when we take responsibility for ourselves, we not only feel better, but the quality of our interaction with others improves dramatically as well. Sometimes taking care of ourselves means saying no. Saying no can be the kindest thing we do for ourselves and others. Saying yes when we need to say no is a form of *rescuing* others. *Rescuing* inevitably leads to self-violation and is not a loving way to treat ourselves.

Saying no becomes easier as our commitment to taking care of ourselves overrides the fear of being rejected or not getting outside approval. It becomes easier because we realize that the only person whose approval we truly need is our own. It's part of making our own well-being our top priority. Saying yes because we don't feel able to say no, is another way of not taking care of ourselves.

When we *rescue*, we feel bad. *Rescuing* leads to feelings like resentment and blame and prompts us to behave like a *persecutor* towards the person we are *rescuing*. Because we do not have a healthy *boundary* with that person, he or she will experience the brunt of the frustration we feel towards ourselves. In other words, when we *rescue*, we hurt ourselves and we *persecute* the other person.

### Exiting the Victim Triangle

When we set healthy *boundaries*, those still living on the *victim triangle* tend to see us as *persecutors*. ("How dare you stop *rescuing*! Who is going to take care of me now?) Taking care of ourselves may cause those who are used to being taken care of at our expense to cry " no fair!" Even though we know we are doing what's best for us both by not *rescuing*, we must be prepared for them to see us as a *persecutor*. They will loudly protest, but we must remember that their protests, no matter how loud, do not make us *persecutors*. As we begin to set *boundaries*, they may complain that we are rejecting or abandoning them. It helps to speak honestly with them in a way that neither justifies, nor devalues, their *personal reality.*

Sometimes our loved ones are deeply invested in verifying their own perception of *Reality* and so opt to stay on the *victim triangle.* We cannot force them to give up their primary way of relating just because we want them to do so, no matter how dysfunctional we may consider their actions. We can share our desire for, and belief in, a different sort of relationship, a relationship free from the *victim triangle.* But beyond that, we must relax into knowing that because we have moved out of *victim consciousness,* our relationship with them is bound to change. Change is inevitable because when one person experiences a shift, the dynamic of the whole relationship changes. When we take responsibility for ourselves and allow others to take responsibility for themselves, our relationship with them will either improve, or it may dissolve. Sometimes dissolution is necessary, but when it is, we find we are ready for it. We find we have the resources available to make the transition from dysfunction to a life of greater health and well-being.

Some of the resources needed for a transition to health come in Step 3 where we learn how to identify and explore the life-restricting beliefs that we have adopted as our *personal reality.*

# CHAPTER FOUR

# Step 3: Our Core Beliefs

We talked at length earlier in the book about *core beliefs*, defining them and explaining how we internalize them. As we make progress, we become increasingly aware of these particular, habitual belief patterns or *core belief* themes that keep us stuck on the *victim triangle*. Our job, in Step 3, is to *observe* these themes closely, so we can take steps to *clear* them.

## *Finding our Core Beliefs*

As we said, life themes that cause us misery are made up of *core beliefs* that create a particular perception of ourselves and the world. Often *core beliefs* appear to parallel each other or correspond to one another. As we will see, they are easily combined in the mind so that, when believed and acted upon, they strengthen and reinforce one another, leading to predictable outcomes. Those outcomes establish the *core beliefs*, at least in our own minds, as *Reality*.

Let's look at an example of how parallel beliefs can combine into a dominating mindset:

Belief 1: "There is not enough to go around. The world is limited."

Belief 2: "People (we)" are not safe. The world is dangerous."

When these two beliefs are combined, the resulting *victim mindset* might be: "I don't have enough. They have more than I do. They can't be trusted. They probably took it from somebody else. I don't trust them. They will try to take what I have. They are dangerous and I must protect myself by taking from them before they attack me."

Combining the belief, "There's not enough" with the parallel belief, "I am not safe," generates a *victim mindset* that, depending upon the degree of conviction with which one holds it, causes fear, resentment, distrust, paranoia, harsh competition, retribution, vindication, and even full-blown attack. It is a classic *starting gate persecutor's* mindset.

Another *victim mindset* altogether, however, is created when the *core belief*, "I don't have enough" is combined with the parallel belief, "They are important/I am not."

The resulting mindset might be: "There is not enough to go around. I can't get what I need. I am not important. I don't matter and therefore will not get what I need. Others are more important than I am. They matter. I need to matter to them to get my needs met. I must take care of them and put them first so I can matter and be important." This *victim mindset* looks more like that of a *starting gate rescuer* on the *victim triangle*.

The consequences of such a *low-frequency* mindset include feelings of guilt, self-sacrifice, fear of unworthiness, inadequacy, martyrdom, resentment, as well as an insatiable drive to be a super caretaker, people-pleaser and the one who knows best. We justify those feelings with the conviction that we have to prove our worth.

When we learn to recognize that symptoms such as misery, resentment, guilt, etc, are caused by *core beliefs* such as the above, we can consciously deal with those symptoms. We learn to see how we have grouped corresponding/parallel beliefs together into limiting life themes/*victim mindsets* that have serious consequences. Only then can we initiate a *clearing* process that addresses/corrects the beliefs and subsequently takes us off of the *victim triangle*.

Step 3 is the process of making our *core beliefs* conscious so we can begin a process of disempowering them and liberating ourselves from a *victim consciousness*. In order to do that we must first identify our *core beliefs*. There are not that many different *core beliefs*. Most of us share one or more of them. (Remember that *core beliefs* lie at the root of a whole series of other more immediately conscious beliefs such as, "They don't appreciate me," "He hates me," "She is mean to me," or "They are trying to hurt me.")

Some of the more common *core beliefs* include the following:

I don't have a right to be here.
I am unlovable.
I am powerless, inadequate, intrinsically flawed.
I can't be helped.
There is something wrong with me.
I am stupid.
I am worthless.
I am a failure.
I am not enough.
I am not safe or protected.
I am a mistake.
I cannot do it right.
My thoughts, feelings, and the way I live my life are unacceptable.
The world is a dangerous place.
Other people cannot be trusted.
I cannot trust myself.

Later on, we will learn how to determine our own particular *core beliefs*. It is worth remembering that having these *core beliefs* does not mean they are *Reality* or the truth. However, when we identify with them, we make them our personal truth. These limiting truths which operate as our *core beliefs* do not have to define us, but that is exactly what they do until we learn to recognize them and then dismantle/correct them.

## *Dismantling our Core Beliefs*

We locate our *core beliefs* by examining any unhappy, stressful thoughts to see what beliefs are at their root. When we find those beliefs, we begin to dismantle them.

Dismantling our limiting *core beliefs*, however, does not mean that we get rid of them! Engaging in efforts to eliminate our troubling *core beliefs* not only feels overwhelming, it is often downright impossible! (I sometimes jokingly tell my clients that my business card does not read, 'Lynne Forrest, Exterminator!') Fortunately we do not have to get rid of our *core beliefs* to gain mental freedom! Simply making our negative beliefs conscious goes a long way towards dismantling them. In the next Chapter, we will learn what to do to dismantle our *core beliefs* once we become conscious of them. But for now, let's look at how to find them.

We start by paying attention to our painful feelings. These *low-frequency* feelings alert us to underlying unhappy thoughts. As we explore our unhappy thoughts, we move through several levels or layers of feelings to find the *core beliefs* at their root.

Here's an example starting with a first-level awareness of a painful feeling:

**First Level:**

Feeling: Outrage

Question: "What thought is generating that feeling?"

**First level of thought:** "How dare he treat me like that! He wouldn't treat anyone else like that."

Result: Feelings of indignation and hurt.

**Second Level:**

Questions: What thought is causing those feelings of indignation and hurt? What am I telling myself?

**Second level of thought:** "I don't matter to him."

Result: Feelings of insignificance.

**Third Level:**

Question: What am I believing that causes those feelings of insignificance?

**Third level of thought:** "I am not important."

Result: Feelings of inadequacy.

**Fourth Level:**

Question: What belief lies behind those feelings of inadequacy?

**Fourth level of thought:** "I am worthless."

Results: Feelings of unimportance and worthlessness.

**Fifth Level:**

Question: What belief is behind those feelings of unimportance and worthlessness?

**Fifth level of thought:** "I don't matter to me."

Result: Feelings of hopelessness.

Since the belief, "I don't matter to me" is self-annihilating, we can call it a *core belief.*

Painful feelings, then, point to distorted beliefs which, in turn, cause unhappiness. Only when we locate and name our distorted beliefs can we change them by *observing* them in a detached manner that restores peace.

We can locate and work with a troubling belief at any level but the most significant shifts in *consciousness* occur when we locate and work with the deeper level of beliefs. When we dismantle the root or *core belief,* we simultaneously dismantle the beliefs related to it and leading to it. (Consider the following apt analogy: when we want to remove a weed from the garden, we may cut it down, or strip it of its branches, but we cannot be sure the weed is really gone unless we kill the roots.)

# CHAPTER FIVE

# The Belief Clearing Process (BCP)

We dismantle our *core beliefs* by using what I shall call a *Belief Clearing Process (BCP)*. We use a *clearing process* to take responsibility for our *low-frequency* beliefs and then use a reliable method to reframe them. We thereby raise our emotional vibration to a *higher frequency*. *Clearing* negative beliefs restores us to *Reality* and peace.

A *Belief Clearing Process (BCP)* is done as needed. We initiate *the BCP* when we recognize we are in a *low-frequency* emotional state and want to feel better.

Just as it is possible to *align* both mentally and physically with *Reality*, it is also possible to *clear* negative beliefs using both body and mind techniques. Both mental and physical techniques for *clearing* are powerful tools for restoring health and well-being. In Chapter 8, we will present an example of *a BCP* using a *body awareness method*. For now, let's examine some *BCPs*.

## Asking the Right Questions

We introduced the importance of asking the right questions earlier in describing a process for locating an underlying *core belief*.

We may remember that the *observer consciousness* is that in us that restores us to *sanity* and peace when we've gotten lost in our unhappy beliefs. And we have already emphasized the importance of asking the right questions in order to locate and reframe a *core belief*. There are particular questions that help activate our *observer consciousness*. Such questions include the following:

What am I telling myself?
What feelings do these thoughts/beliefs generate?
Are my feelings of a *high* or *low-frequency*?

What thoughts lie behind those feelings?

What am I *projecting*? (What am I blaming others for?)

How am I not taking responsibility for myself right now?

What do I need to do to take responsibility for?

What are the underlying beliefs behind this thought?

Writing down our answers to these questions helps immensely. *Victim consciousness* easily distracts us, and keeps us from staying on point when we try to do the process in our minds. By writing our thoughts down we focus because writing, by its very nature, forces us to put all the powers of the mind on the questions we ask ourselves.

We must look for the underlying belief that is prompting our behavior so we can assess the validity of that belief and its impact on us. As we've said before, it does not help to judge or *resist* our thoughts/beliefs: what works better is to see these less-than-pleasing thoughts/beliefs with humor and appreciation. We must be explicitly honest with ourselves if we expect to *clear* them. Telling ourselves the truth and not judging ourselves makes it possible for us to *align* with *Reality*. Only then can we understand and appreciate the lessons they teach. Self-forgiveness and freedom from *victim consciousness* are the results.

We cannot simply get rid of unhealthy thoughts/beliefs by ordering them out of our lives. The old saying, "like attracts like," is based on a universal principle that teaches that what we focus our attention on expands. In other words, the more we focus on eliminating a troublesome thought, the more it haunts us.

*Resistance*, of any kind, does not work. When we hate something about ourselves, we cannot get rid of that something because hate, and its consequence - judgment - is a form of *resistance* that continues to attract *low-frequency*, vibrational energy. In other words, the more we hate, and as a result, judge something, the bigger the problem becomes. The old saying, "What we *resist* persists," is true!

Rather than *resisting*, or fighting unwanted thoughts/beliefs, we step back from them, step into *observer consciousness* instead, and question them. The acts of *observing* these thoughts/beliefs and asking the right questions about them dissolves *resistance* because they allow us to detach. As a result, troublesome thoughts/beliefs diminish on their own; we don't have to order them out of our lives. We become detached from the beliefs that were causing us trouble, allowing us to see things differently. Detachment frees us from the mental state of *victim consciousness*. The more prompt we are in *observing* and questioning our unhappy beliefs, the more quickly we release the false stories that hold us captive on the *victim triangle*, and the more quickly we gain peace.

When we bring our *low-frequency* beliefs/thoughts to *consciousness*, *observe* them, and step back to question them, we avoid their pitfalls. It's as if we are walking down a street and suddenly come upon a deep, foul-smelling pile of rot. Sensing and seeing the foul-smelling pile, we naturally step around it to avoid it. We don't want it on our shoes! Similarly, through *observer consciousness*, we see the *low-frequency* quality of certain thoughts/beliefs; we recognize the distress they produce and we question them. We then deliberately choose to ignore them (avoid them) rather than soil ourselves with them. In so doing, we give them no energy; we starve them and they wither, leaving us in peace.

## *Introducing Three BCP Methods*

There are three methods that work effectively to dismantle stressful *core beliefs*. It is these three methods that constitute the *BCP* that I personally use to maintain my own inner balance, peace and well-being. Using this *BCP*, many of my clients, over the past ten to fifteen years, have freed themselves from *victim consciousness* and gained inner peace and a significantly higher quality of life.

I developed the first method in the *BCP*, the *Core Belief Cycle*™ *(CBC)*, over years of working with clients in one on one, group and workshop settings (p. 96).

The second method in the *BCP* was developed by Byron Katie (2002). This method employs four questions and what she calls turnarounds, which are a way of experiencing the opposite of what you believe. (Katie's simple yet profound process called The Work is the most powerful formula I have found to neutralize negative *core beliefs*.)

The third method, *body awareness* and *clearing*, is my newest addition to the *BCP*. It is a method by which the physical body becomes the primary vessel for transformation. By understanding that physical pain is directly linked to limiting beliefs stored in the body, we can *clear* old beliefs using *body awareness methods*, in combination with physical activities such as yoga and *qigong*.

*Body awareness methods* are based on understanding that our body creates a pattern of contraction in response to our limiting thoughts/beliefs. That pattern of contraction eventually leads to physical problems and pain. If we believe we are not safe, for instance, our bodies will store fear in certain areas of our body. By exploring such areas of physical contraction in the body, we can uncover the belief that is behind the discomfort or pain and *clear* it so that balance can be restored and physical rejuvenation and healing can take place.

I highly recommend utilizing these three methods. Any one of them brings insight and relief, but when used together, the *BCP* become a holistic approach that takes into consideration our whole self, mentally, emotionally and physically. The nature and amount of effort we use in applying these methods to *clear* our minds and bodies of negative beliefs determine the quality of our results.

# CHAPTER SIX

# BCP Method 1: The Core Belief Cycle™

I developed the *Core Belief Cycle*™(CBC) as a map or a tool for understanding our own *core beliefs*. Until we can recognize and *observe* our *core beliefs* in action, we cannot effectively dismantle them. As previously emphasized, our *core beliefs* are what fuel our negative feelings and behavior. These limited behavioral and emotional *reactions*, along with the beliefs behind them, come together to create a specific and particular pattern that becomes our own personal *Core Belief Cycle*™ *(CBC)*.

As previously described, we go through the *CBC* over and over based on our own perception of *unmet needs*. That perception prompts us to make *negative life decisions* that harden into particular *core beliefs*. Those particular *core beliefs* cause us painful feelings that lead to either *victim, persecutor, or rescuer defenses*. Those *defenses* reinforce our *core belief* and so the cycle begins anew.

At the risk of stating the obvious: life affirming beliefs do not drive our *CBC*. Our limiting, unhappy beliefs do! They perpetuate the *CBC* that imprison us on the *victim triangle*.

*Core beliefs* originate out of *unmet needs* (at the bottom of the circle) and *negative family messages* perceived in childhood (follow the arrows). Those painfully limiting messages from family members prompt us to make *negative life decisions* that, once accepted, become *core beliefs* that are often never again questioned. These unhappy *core beliefs* generate painful feelings that we then medicate through *defenses* we acquire to protect ourselves. The latter shape our self-image or *persona*. The *negative consequences*, as well as *negative payoffs*, that come from living out of our *defenses* keep us hooked on the *CBC* in a continuing downward spiral.

# CORE BELIEF CYCLE

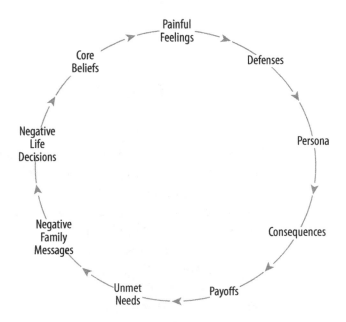

(See Glossary for special definitions of the words in italics.)

The *CBC* diagram defines our personal habitual progression through a sequence of limiting beliefs, unhappy feelings, and painful *defenses*. *Defenses* (p. 104) determine our behavior, and our behavior determines how we are perceived. Starting with *unmet needs*, the *CBC* prompts us to act out painful or *negative life decisions* that originated in childhood and that continue to manifest in our daily lives. In other words, the *CBC* is a map of sorts outlining the obstacles/stumbling blocks we create for ourselves in our day-to-day life.

*Core beliefs* are triggered when we perceive that our needs are not being met. Feeling deprived of something vital to our well-being, like safety, acceptance, belonging, permission to be, etc., threatens our sense of self, and sets us up for our *CBC*. This means we *react* out of a *negative life decision* we made as children about the futility of meeting a particular need. We choose, yet again, the same limiting *negative life decision*, and in that way we reinforce the underlying *core belief*. The result is painful feelings that often prompt an eruption of *defensive reactions* which, in turn, have their own backlash effect. We prove to ourselves, once more, that our original *negative life decisions*, and their underlying *core beliefs* are true. We repeat this cycle endlessly, playing out our particular pattern on the *victim triangle*. We are powerless over this cycle until o*bserver consciousness* intervenes.

*Observer consciousness* identifies our cyclic pattern. Only then can we begin Step 2 of the *clearing* method: questioning our *core beliefs*. But we have to know what our own individual *CBC* is before we can dismantle it and get ourselves off of the *victim triangle*.

## Studying Sally's Example

Discovering what our *core beliefs* are and how we react when they are triggered is an important part of our recovery from v*ictim consciousness*. Although we may be able, using step 2 of the *clearing process*, to successfully dismantle unhappy thoughts and limiting beliefs and find relief from them, we will stay mired in the dynamics of v*ictim consciousness* until we know our own *core beliefs*. It is our *core beliefs* that hold our negative belief system in place.

The purpose of this section is to learn how to map our own *Core Belief Cycle*™ *(CBC)*. We use Sally's story as our case example to illustrate the *CBC*. Sally is a composite of the clients I have worked with and her story is a composite of the stories I have heard repeatedly in my practice. By following the process I set forth here, and by replacing Sally's answers and examples with your own answers and examples, you can determine your own *CBC*.

With pen and paper, let's explore Sally's *CBC*. As I ask Sally these questions, you may want to respond with your own answers.

I start by asking Sally to think back to a childhood event that took place within her family, an event that she considered to be a painfully defining moment for herself, and to write it down.

Sally writes the following memory:

I was five years old, and had gone to bed when, suddenly my dad comes storming into the room, flips on the overhead light, and jerks me, bodily, out of the bed. He is mad. He is yelling at me because I forgot to put the milk back in the refrigerator. Mom is standing in the doorway behind him, her hands on her hips and she looks mad too. He tells me I am stupid, selfish, and ungrateful for all they do for me. He is shaking me hard as he yells at me. I am terrified and crying, saying, "I'm sorry daddy, I won't do it again," but he doesn't act like he hears me. Instead he slaps my face, and flings me back on the bed, as if I were a rag doll, saying, "You don't deserve to eat the food in this house - I am sick and tired of your selfish, wasteful ways, and I will flail the life out of you if you ever do it again." He then turns and storms out, slamming the door behind him.

I lie there, wide awake, paralyzed with fear that he might come back. I lie there, frantically trying to remember what other bad things I might have done that day that might make him come after me again. What was worse was, I couldn't remember having left the milk out at all! I was sure, as a matter of fact, that I HAD NOT left it out. This meant either I was crazy, or so forgetful that I couldn't trust myself not to have done something else just as bad that would be discovered any minute.

## Components of the CBC

### Unmet Needs

Next, I say to Sally, "You experienced a painful and difficult situation. Determine what your *unmet needs* and wants were as you went through that situation and write them down." Sally lists the following:

"I needed to feel safe."

"I wanted to be understood."

"I wanted to be spoken to with respect."

"I wanted to tell my side of the story."

"I wanted to be heard and believed."

"I needed to feel important to my parents."

"I needed permission to make mistakes."

"I wanted forgiveness."

"I longed to know that I wasn't bad because I'd made a mistake."

"I needed to know that everyone makes mistakes."

## My (Sally's) Core Belief Cycle

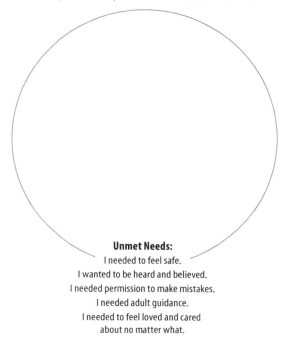

**Unmet Needs:**
I needed to feel safe.
I wanted to be heard and believed.
I needed permission to make mistakes.
I needed adult guidance.
I needed to feel loved and cared
about no matter what.

"I needed protection from dad's anger and rage."

"I needed adult guidance."

"I needed to feel loved and cared about no matter what."

Since all *core beliefs* originate in *unmet needs*, we place those *unmet needs* first on our personal *CBC*.

As illustrated in the diagram above, draw a similar, large circle and place your own list of *unmet needs* at the bottom of the circle.

### Negative Family Messages

I then ask Sally the following question: "What were the *negative family messages*, verbal and implied, you received from those involved in your childhood memory?" Write them down.

Here are the *negative family messages* Sally lists that she received from her parents:

"It's your fault that we are angry."

"You are to blame for our behavior."

"We are in control."

"Your safety and well-being do not matter to us."

"We don't care how you feel."

"Our feelings (anger) are more important to us than your needs for rest/sleep."

"You are at our mercy."

"You are bad and do not deserve to eat."

"You have to be perfect to be accepted, even to stay alive, perhaps."

"You are not perfect, therefore you are unacceptable and will be punished."

"You are irretrievably wrong."

"You are selfish and wasteful, and therefore undeserving of our love."

"You cannot be trusted."

"We are right, you are wrong."

"We are not interested in hearing your thoughts or opinions."

"We don't believe you."

"We can and will hurt you."

Following Sally's example, list the *negative family messages* that you received from your childhood situation. Place them to the left of *Unmet Needs* under the heading, *Negative Family Messages*, like the diagram on the next page.

### Negative Life Decisions

Like Sally, the *negative family messages* we heard, implied or spoken, from significant caregivers strongly influenced the *negative life decisions* we made about ourselves and the world. Such *negative life decisions* set the tone for the way we continue to relate to ourselves and the world around us. Such decisions, once made, are rarely questioned. They become ours for life unless we make them conscious and question them. We blindly believe them and, as a result, we act in such a way that we devalue ourselves in our own minds.

It is common for us, as children, to believe that whatever happens to us is about us, is caused by us. We often presume that

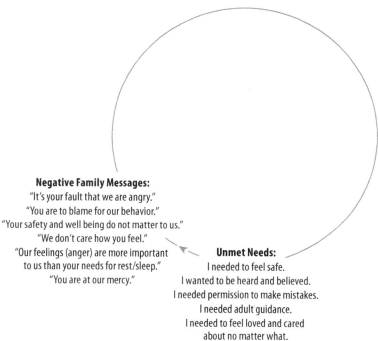

**Negative Family Messages:**
"It's your fault that we are angry."
"You are to blame for our behavior."
"Your safety and well being do not matter to us."
"We don't care how you feel."
"Our feelings (anger) are more important
to us than your needs for rest/sleep."
"You are at our mercy."

**Unmet Needs:**
I needed to feel safe.
I wanted to be heard and believed.
I needed permission to make mistakes.
I needed adult guidance.
I needed to feel loved and cared
about no matter what.

others treat us the way they do because it's how we deserve to be treated. However, the way parents behave towards us is not based on what we are worth or what we deserve. This fact is easy to understand when we remember that people act the way they do because of what they are thinking and believing, not because of what others are doing or saying!

It is our beliefs, not external conditions, that generate our feelings and behavior. It is the assumptions and unquestioned beliefs that parents have about their children that cause them to interact with their children as they do. They forget or do not fully understand the child's intrinsic value and worth! When we, as children, believe that our treatment at the hands of others is what we deserve, it affects our sense of self-worth and ends up reflecting what we believe our parents thought. We assume that if others treat us well, it must be because we are good and deserving, or at least, behaving properly. And, using that child logic, we also believe that if we are not being treated well, it is because we are bad, undeserving, and/or behaving improperly. The *negative life decisions* of our *CBC* then, are based on misguided thinking: our parents misguided thinking first and subsequently our own. We buy into the messages we receive from parents who are themselves living on the *victim triangle* and are therefore unable to encourage us towards healthier life decisions.

To determine some of her own *negative life decisions*, I ask Sally the following question:

"In response to the *negative family messages* you received, what did you decide about yourself, others, and the world around you?"

Write down those *negative life decisions*. Sally writes the following:

"I am never safe."

" I am at the mercy of those bigger, stronger and more powerful than me."

"I am bad and deserve to be punished."

"I must be perfect to be acceptable, otherwise I will be rejected and punished."

"Love hurts and acceptance is impossible."

"Their unhappiness is my fault."

"My feelings, thoughts, opinions, needs, and wants do not matter."

"I am selfish and wasteful and undeserving."

"I cannot trust myself to be right."

"I cannot trust others to be reliable or safe."

"People are dangerous."

"My home is not safe, therefore there is nowhere that is safe."

"I do not deserve protection."

"Nobody cares about me."

"Things (like milk) are more important than I am."

"I am worthless."

Write down your own comparable list as follows: On the diagram of your own *CBC*, write the heading, *Negative life decisions* and list (in small print) your decisions related to the memory you are working on in the *CBC* diagram above the heading, *Negative Family Messages.*

## Sally's *Core Belief*

Our *core beliefs* come from painful, often unconscious, and *negative life decisions* like those Sally lists above, that we store in our psyche. Such *core beliefs* are often fixed by the time we are four or five years old and they will continue to dictate the success and happiness we experience in life unless and until we find them and change them. We don't even recognize we have these *core beliefs*, much less suspect that they control our responses to life.

Our *core beliefs* are a composite of several of the *negative life decisions* we listed earlier. Those beliefs define who we are and what we can expect from life. Not surprisingly, Sally's *core belief* is as follows: "I am unlovable and unacceptable because I am imperfect. I don't deserve to be protected or loved."

Write down your *core belief* on your *CBC*. Write it on the top left side of a large circle, like this:

## Painful Feelings

Our *core beliefs* generate painful feelings every time any situation reminds us, consciously or unconsciously, of our original childhood trauma. I now ask Sally to list the painful feelings that her *core beliefs* generated. Here is her list:

Fear
Worthlessness
Sadness, Depression
Hopelessness
Unimportance
Lack of safety, lack of protection
Rejection
Anxiety
Hurt

## My (Sally's) Core Belief Cycle

**Core Beliefs:**
"I am unlovable and unacceptable
because I am imperfect.
I don't deserve to be protected or loved."

**Negative Life Decisions:**
"I am never safe."
"I am bad and deserve to be punished."
"I must be perfect to be acceptable.
Otherwise I will be rejected and punished."
"Love hurts and acceptance is impossible."
"Their unhappiness is my fault."
"My feelings, thoughts, opinions,
needs, and wants do not matter."
"I cannot trust myself to be right."

**Negative Family Messages:**
"It's your fault that we are angry."
"You are to blame for our behavior."
"Your safety and well being do not matter to us."
"We don't care how you feel."
"Our feelings (anger) are more important
to us than your needs for rest/sleep."
"You are at our mercy."

**Unmet Needs:**
I needed to feel safe.
I wanted to be heard and believed.
I needed permission to make mistakes.
I needed adult guidance.
I needed to feel loved and cared
about no matter what.

## Defenses

Because nothing moves us faster than does discomfort, painful feelings motivate us to take action promptly. Rather than question our *core beliefs*, we instead devise creative ways to avoid those painful feelings by either stuffing, denying, or medicating them. We call these ways of dealing with our uncomfortable feelings and *core beliefs*, *defenses*. List yours on the *CBC* after your *core belief*.

Next I ask Sally to write about her *defenses* and to underline those parts she thinks are *defensive* behaviors. She writes the following:

"<u>I avoid getting close to others,</u> as a way of keeping people from knowing how worthless and undeserving I am. I <u>don't ask for what I need</u> because I am not worth it. <u>I do it all myself</u> instead, and <u>never ask for help</u>. I <u>work hard to please others</u> so they won't reject me and <u>I take responsibility for the feelings of others,</u> because I believe their happiness/unhappiness is my responsibility. I believe

I must earn acceptance by being perfect. I believe I have to be right to stay safe and I will do anything to avoid conflict because I am afraid of being hurt. I avoid intimacy because if I get too attached to people I expect to be rejected. I don't trust anyone. I avoid confrontation and "never make waves." I avoid anger, and go along with others even when I do not agree. I stuff my feelings with alcohol, work, and food, and I hide my resentment, hurt, and frustration behind a smile to cover up how bad I feel about myself. I tell people what they want to hear, rather than telling the truth because what I think doesn't matter anyway. I avoid taking risks. I play it safe instead. I have to be in control at all times of myself and my life situation to prevent being hurt by those who will reject me. After all, I am worthless and will be rejected or punished sooner or later."

I ask Sally to review what she has written and to make a simple list of *defenses*. Here is her list:

I isolate myself.
I avoid intimacy.
I deny my needs.
I stuff my feelings, especially my anger.
I medicate myself with food and alcohol.
I stay busy.
I hide behind my work.
I am a perfectionist.
I avoid confrontation and conflict of any kind.
I hide my uncomfortable feelings behind a smile.
I am a people-pleaser.
I always try to fit in and be like those around me.
I never let my guard down.
I force myself to appear in charge and well-controlled.
I have to be in charge.
I need to be the expert.
I cannot take risks.
I do what is expected of me.

## Persona

Our *defenses* come together to form a shield of protection or mask, behind which we hide our vulnerability; such a mask affords us an illusion of safety in what otherwise feels to be an unsafe world. Psychologists often refer to this defensive mask as our *persona*, a self-made identity mistakenly assumed, by ourselves and others, to be who we are. It is really a false identity that we create out of our limited beliefs about ourselves.

The *persona* is also commonly referred to as our personality. In other words, the *persona* is a manifestation of the thoughts/beliefs/feelings/*defenses* that we listed on our *CBC*. This packaged and false identity or self that we create out of our *defenses* is who we have come to think we are! Let's use Sally's *persona* as a model to help us determine the nature of our own *persona*. We note her *defenses* **in Bold.**

Sally is a divorcée who lives alone. She is a top executive assistant for the CEO of a large company and she is **very good at what she does.** She is **self sufficient** - to a fault. She **works constantly** and even her social life revolves around work. She is a **natural organizer and event planner** and **others rely on her** skills in that area.

But Sally **avoids intimacy** with everyone. She especially avoids men since her divorce ten years ago (her former husband had become increasingly angry and verbally abusive). She dates occasionally, but **prefers a solitary home-life.** She does have a few good friends from work whom she sees at regular times each week. Sally **prefers routines** and **doesn't like surprises.** She **hates confrontation** and fears rejection. As a result, she mostly **goes along with what others want,** even when what they want is not what she wants.

Although Sally **always smiles** on the outside, she rarely smiles on the inside. She is too busy **finding fault with herself and others.** She is **detail oriented** and **hyper-vigilant** and habitually **visualizes the worst case scenario** in every situation. Although she doesn't gossip about her friends and acquaintances, she does **judge them negatively,** using her list of imperfections/faults. She uses those negative judgments as reasons to **avoid taking risks** and to **avoid getting too close** to her friends.

Sally **prefers to be home** where she can take off her mask. She likes **to be alone** because she can watch TV, **drink** a few glasses of wine and **eat sweets** without having to please anybody or risk their criticism. These evening respites are Sally's chief way of relaxing.

The above portrayal describes Sally's *persona*. It describes the false self that her *core belief* has created. As long as Sally is caught in that cycle, she cannot express her *authentic self*. She can only express what her *core belief* dictates: "**I am unlovable and unacceptable because I am imperfect. I don't deserve to be protected or loved.**" That *core belief* dictates how she makes decisions and how she reacts to life's circumstances.

Our *starting gate position* on the *victim triangle* is also part of our *persona*. Our personal *core beliefs* determine what role on the *triangle* we are best suited to play (*victim, persecutor, rescuer*). For instance, being at the mercy of a *core belief* that says she does not deserve to be loved, Sally routinely denies her own needs. Instead of taking care of herself she seeks validation and a sense of importance by taking care of others. In other words, Sally's *core belief* sets her up as a *starting gate rescuer*.

To discover our own *persona* we must explore important questions, such as, "How does my *core belief* define me? What are the feelings and *defenses* that accompany my *core beliefs*?" "How do others see me?"

As we examine each of the lists in our *CBC*, we can see how our *defenses,* feelings and *negative life decisions* have all come together to form the identity we call "me," but which, in truth, is not who we are at all, but is instead a mask, or *persona*, merely the program of habitual feelings and reactions triggered by our own internalized beliefs.

Make your own list, similar to Sally's list below, and add it on your personal *CBC* under the word *Persona*. Here are the characteristics Sally listed regarding how others might describe her *persona*:

## My (Sally's) Core Belief Cycle

**Painful Feelings:**
Fear
Worthlessness
Sadness, Depression
Hopelessness
Unimportance
Unsafe
Rejection
Anxiety
Hurt

**Core Beliefs:**
"I am unlovable and unacceptable
because I am imperfect.
I don't deserve to be protected or loved."

**My Defenses:**
I isolate myself.
I avoid intimacy.
I deny my needs.
I stuff my feelings, especially anger.
I medicate myself with food and alcohol.
I stay busy.
I hide behind my work.
I am a perfectionist.

**Negative Life Decisions:**
"I am never safe."
"I am bad and deserve to be punished."
"I must be perfect to be acceptable.
Otherwise I will be rejected and punished."
"Love hurts and acceptance is impossible."
"Their unhappiness is my fault."
"My feelings, thoughts, opinions,
needs, and wants do not matter."
"I cannot trust myself to be right."

**Persona:**
Others see me as a hard worker,
possibly as workaholic.
I am seen as independent,
often as a loner.
I am seen as detail oriented,
a good organizer, as a controller.
I am seen as hard to get to know
or get close to.
I am seen as a perfectionist
and as a people-pleaser.

**Negative Family Messages:**
"It's your fault that we are angry."
"You are to blame for our behavior."
"Your safety and well being do not matter to us."
"We don't care how you feel."
"Our feelings (anger) are more important
to us than your needs for rest/sleep."
"You are at our mercy."

**Payoffs/Negative Consequences:**
Emotional safety/Isolation
Approval from others/ Self-neglect
Sense of belonging/Loss of personal freedom
Sense of accomplishment/Work-driven
Career advancement/Loss of connection
w/ self and others

**Unmet Needs:**
I needed to feel safe.
I wanted to be heard and believed.
I needed permission to make mistakes.
I needed adult guidance.
I needed to feel loved and cared
about no matter what.

Sally looks good. She appears competent and happy.

Sally seems highly skilled and efficient.

Sally is a hard worker. She may be a workaholic.

Sally is independent.

Sally is always in control.

Sally can be very controlling.

Sally is a problem solver and solution finder.

Sally is well organized and a good company organizer.

Sally is aloof and hard to get to know.

Sally seems a bit rigid or isolated from others.

Sally is a perfectionist. She is obsessed with details.

Sally is a people pleaser.

Sally is a career woman who chooses work over family.

## Negative Consequences

When we believe our *core beliefs*, we *react defensively* and experience the accompanying, painful *negative consequences*. There is no way we can live out of our *core belief* without experiencing *negative consequences*. When we believe limited ideas about who we are, we suffer from some, or all, of the following: poor self-esteem, chronic depression, worry/anxiety, paranoia, isolation, troubled relationships, deep seated resentments, self-neglect, and outright self-hatred. These conditions/symptoms are the *negative consequences* of neglecting our *authentic selves* by living from our *core beliefs*, and to distrust and judge others, instead.

We think of these *negative consequences* as problems we need to fix or eliminate. We eagerly look for quick fixes, spending millions of dollars every year seeking relief from them through superficial, band-aid style remedies. We spend money on everything from spa treatments to anti-depressants, dating services, crash courses on communication, mindless entertainment or promoting good causes, not to mention the money we spend on various kinds of therapy. What we fail to realize is that our problems are the result of our *CBCs*, and therefore cannot be truly remedied until we address the underlying *core beliefs* that cause them.

*Negative consequences* are the price we pay for life on the *victim triangle*. To help Sally determine the *negative consequences* of her *core beliefs* and *defenses*, I asked her to address the following questions:

> What are the *negative consequences* of living out of my *CBC*?
>
> How does *reacting* out of my *defenses* and *core beliefs* affect my self image?
>
> How does my *CBC* affect my relationships with others?
>
> What compulsive behaviors/addictions do I practice as a result?
>
> How does living on the *CBC* affect my health?
>
> How does it affect my spiritual life?
>
> How does it limit my ability to manifest the life I want?

For Sally, becoming aware of the *negative consequences* she experiences from living her *core belief* ("I am unimportant and unlovable") helps her to respond in a more healthy manner when her feelings and *defenses* are activated. She feels less compelled to *react* in ways that would cause those familiar and uncomfortable *negative consequences*. For instance, her *defenses* often prompt Sally to avoid people. As a result, she suffers from a lack of validation and intimacy. Her fear of taking risks keeps her safe maybe, but severely limits her creative self-expression. Such *negative consequences* reinforce Sally's *unmet needs* (to feel important, connected, loved, and valued) and reinforce and perpetuate her *core belief* ("I am unimportant and unlovable").

Write your answers thoughtfully and honestly. Doing so will help you not only to determine the *negative consequences* of your *core beliefs*, but will also help you to come to terms with those *negative consequences*.

Here is Sally's list of *negative consequences*:

Loss of self-respect: low self esteem.

Emotional and physical exhaustion

Distrust of others

Isolation

Loss of connection with self, others, and Source

Confused identity (for example: "who am I?")

Loss of social life

Weight gain (compulsive overeater)

Alcohol abuse, hangovers

Work addiction

High blood pressure

Lost opportunities for adventure and growth

Resentment and envy of others

Depression

Dissatisfaction and general unhappiness

Her list could go on and on. Your list of *negative consequences* almost completes your *CBC*. But there is one more category left to explore; it is the category of *payoffs*. *Payoffs* are often overlooked; the *negative consequences* are more obvious and often overshadow the benefits (often false) that come from practicing our *defenses*. Nonetheless the *payoffs* are a big part of the reason we stay stuck in our *CBC*.

## Payoffs

Our *defenses* not only bring *negative consequences*; they bring perceived positive *payoffs* as well. These *payoffs* validate and reinforce our *CBC*, causing us to think that our *defenses* are working for us. Our *defenses* serve us in important ways. If they did not, we would not tolerate their *negative consequences*!

Sally, for instance, avoids intimacy, even though doing so leaves her feeling disconnected and alone, because she believes avoiding intimacy protects her from the emotional pain of rejection. By being a perfectionist and people-pleaser, she wins approval from others and a short-lived sense of accomplishment. These *payoffs* compensate temporarily for the lack of self-worth she suffers.

Just as Sally's *defenses* provide *payoffs* for her unconscious feelings of inadequacy, our *defenses* serve us too. They provide the illusion that our *unmet needs* are being met. They give us a sense of safety in what otherwise feels to be a very unsafe world. However *payoffs* provide a false sense of security at best; they do not truly meet our physical/emotional needs for safety, belonging, validation, etc. Our *defenses* only reinforce our *unmet needs*. Meanwhile we suffer the *negative consequences* and verify the *core beliefs* that originated in those *unmet needs*.

If we do not become fully conscious of the nature of our *defenses*, we continue to blindly practice them because of the *payoffs* we think they provide for us, and we become more enslaved to our *CBC*. For that reason, it is wise to fully investigate the nature of our *defenses*. We must investigate both the perceived *payoffs* and their *negative consequences* as a step towards finding more effective strategies for meeting our needs.

Here is Sally's list of *payoffs* and a list of parallel *negative consequences* from her *defenses*:

Emotional safety—Isolation

Personal space/*boundaries*—Emotional distance/walls

Approval from others—Self-neglect and loss of self respect
Sense of belonging—Loss of personal freedom
Sense of accomplishment—Career possessed and driven
Respect from others—Loss of self-respect/loss of self
Job security—Undeveloped personal creativity
Career advancement—Loss of connection w/ self and others
Sense of purpose—Confusion about one's life purpose
Feeling indispensable/important—Feeling unappreciated/resentful

Write your own list of *payoffs* and your own list of parallel *negative consequences* and place them on your *CBC* at the bottom of your circle. Refer to your list of *unmet needs* and notice how your *payoffs* attempt to compensate for the *unmet needs*. Notice also how your *negative consequences* reinforce your *unmet needs*! Finally, notice how your *negative consequences* reinforce your *core belief*!

The *CBC* forms a circle that continues to spiral down into *victim consciousness*. That's why we call it a *core belief cycle*. The obvious question is, "How do we stop this downward spiral?" The answer lies in addressing our emotions. They are the key to identifying our *core belief*. We must engage in a *BCP (belief clearing process)*.

## *Getting Off of the CBC*

There is an exit from this downward, spiraling *CBC (core belief cycle)*. It can be found through our painful feelings. As previously established, our feelings play an essential part in the *clearing process* (pp. 12 & 13). Getting off the *victim triangle* entails putting that information to work for us. We must relate in a totally different way to our "feeling" life. We begin to understand that painful feelings are signals/messages/warnings; they show us the way off of the *victim triangle*.

They do so in unexpected ways: going deeper into them, releasing them, or reliving them. We must see them as signals/messages/warnings informing us of the *low-frequency* of our thoughts. We must not indulge them. This understanding is important.

To ignore or deny our painful feelings and to proceed only on what we think and believe is to be as stuck in *victim consciousness* as it is to indulge in painful feelings without seeking their mental source. Without input from our feelings we cannot tell when we are in, or out, of *alignment* with *Reality*. We need the emotional body; we depend upon it (our feelings) to let us know when we are enslaved by a negative *core belief*.

We learn to pay immediate attention when our feelings signal that we are in emotional distress, no matter how trivial the distress may seem. The point is to *observe* feelings, rather than to wallow in them. When we move into *observer consciousness*, we *witness* our feelings with detached acceptance, allowing them to lead us to the *core beliefs* which are the source of our unhappiness. Indulging painful feelings or wallowing in them holds us back from a genuine peace and a purer connection with *Source*.

When we understand how our emotional body functions, we use our feelings to find *low-frequency* beliefs/thoughts, to adjust/change those beliefs/thoughts, and thus raise our overall *emotional frequency*. Rather than being at the mercy of painful feelings, we use them to alert us to when we are thinking *low-frequency* thoughts, and then we can act to change the *core belief* that gives rise to those thoughts. In other words, we *clear* the *core belief* that is causing the *low-frequency* feelings and act to restore our sense of peace and well-being. This is what an appropriate balance between the emotional and mental bodies looks like. The two work together to bring us into a greater and deeper connection with *Source*.

When we are operating from a *low-frequency* with its attendant painful feelings (hurt, anger, fear, rejection, betrayal, etc), we have a choice. We can choose to move into our old *defenses*, or we can choose to reverse the *CBC* and move towards freedom.

Reversing the *CBC* means we turn our attention away from our *victim mindset* and instead focus on exploring the *core beliefs* that keep us there. Rather than *react* to the external situation from our old *defenses*, we instead look within for mental/emotional clarity. We shift our focus away from blaming something out there, and instead look inside our own minds for the limiting belief that is causing our painful feelings. That simple shift in focus changes everything.

Anytime we feel unhappy, resentful, ashamed, guilty, depressed, anxious, or worried, it is our emotional body signaling that *victim consciousness* is in charge. Painful feelings indicate a *low-frequency* state of *consciousness*. These feelings are not bad or wrong; they simply inform us that our *victim consciousness* is creating unhappy thoughts. Becoming intimately familiar with our *CBC* helps us to recognize when we are in *victim consciousness* so we can initiate a process of transformation.

Our goal is to get off the *victim triangle*, to free ourselves from *victim consciousness*. We have come to see that our feelings are messengers, but they do not necessarily tell us what *Reality* is. They report what our personal mental/*emotional frequency* is in the moment. Our feelings tell us what the *emotional frequency* of our thoughts are, and with that understanding we forge a powerful collaboration with our emotional body. That collaboration is not a relationship where our emotions dictate the quality of our life, but one where we listen closely to our feelings to determine where we are out of *alignment* with *Source*. The emotional body becomes a good friend telling us plainly when we not *aligned* with *Source*.

We have been taking an in-depth look at defining and exploring the *Core Belief Cycle (CBC)* as the first method in the *belief clearing process (BCP)*. Let's now examine the second method I recommend.

# CHAPTER SEVEN

# BCP Method 2:
# Byron Katie's "The Work"

Once we are familiar with the nature of our own *CBC* we must move on to the next step: freeing ourselves from our *core beliefs*. *Clearing* our *core beliefs* does not mean we get rid of them; that may not even be possible. However, we can distance ourselves from them through a process of questioning them. When we can stand back from our pain-producing *core beliefs,* we are no longer at their mercy. Once we stop fueling our *core beliefs* with negative *reactions*, they lose power over us. When we withdraw our attention from them, they wither on the vine from lack of attention. Detached *observation* with an attitude of curious inquiry is the key. We move from a *victim consciousness* to an *observer consciousness*.

Byron Katie's inquiry process, simply called The Work, (Katie, 2002) is an effective and powerful method for making that move. The Work consists of four direct and very simple questions and includes what Katie calls turnarounds. (Read <u>Loving What Is</u>, by Byron Katie. Check www.thework.com).

Katie's simple yet profound process allows us to access our *observer consciousness* so that we can *clear* our *core beliefs*. That is why I decided to include "The Work" here as a vital resource in the *BCP*. It is very beneficial in helping to question and *clear* the beliefs and life assumptions that cause grief. Through The Work, we learn to look closely at assumptions we never thought to question and, by so doing, we restore our *sanity* and peace of mind. Presented below is a description of Byron Katie's valuable set of tools.

## Learning the Four Questions

Byron Katie suggests we ask ourselves the following four questions whenever we locate a troubling thought or belief (Katie, 2002):

1. Is it true?
2. Can you absolutely know that it's true?
3. How do you react, what happens, when you believe that thought?
4. Who would you be without that thought?

To make best use of Katie's The Work, we must first locate the thought that is causing us stress and write it down. We then reflect on it as we ask four questions, starting with the first:

1. Is it true? When I ask this question, I am not looking for the absolute right answer, or trying to give the answer I think I should give. I am simply answering the question according to what I really, truly believe. It is important to commit to a definite yes or no. Leave off the qualifiers and rationale; I either believe it is true, or I do not. Choose. If I find myself adding a "but" or "because," I know that I have left The Work. I stop doing The Work whenever I justify or defend my thoughts. I bring myself back to The Work with a simple "yes" or "no." I know I can always change my mind later. If the answer to this first question is no, I move on to the third question. If the answer is yes, I ask the second question, which is as follows:

2. Can I absolutely know that it's true? This question allows me to take my thought process deeper. It provides me with an opportunity to reflect, to meditate on my belief. Do I know, beyond a shadow of doubt, that the thought I am questioning is true? Once I've answered with a definite yes or no, I move on to question three:

3. How do I react, what happens, when I believe that thought? (Remember, what we believe affects how we feel and act.) This question is designed to show me my *reactions* when I believe a particular thought. When I

believe the thought "I'm not good enough," for example, what do I feel in my body? Is there any discomfort or contraction? Where do I feel that specifically? What emotions do I feel when I believe this thought? Sadness, depression, hopelessness, fear? I am specific in my answers. What images of myself do I see? How do I treat myself when I believe this thought? How do I treat others?

As I continue investigating my *core belief*, I notice an increased sense of detachment from it. This is the power of *observation* at work. Through inquiry I become less *reactive* because I am aware of how believing the thought causes me to act in ways that verify it.

This question prompts me to look at exactly how I behave towards others, at how my choices throughout the day are influenced, and at how I feel about myself when I believe the thought in question. Once I've written the details of who I am as a result of believing my thought, I ask question four.

4. Who would I be without that thought? When asking this question, I am not implying that I shouldn't believe the thought, nor am I suggesting that I can stop believing it; I am simply taking a moment to look at how, who, or what I would be if I didn't believe that thought, if I didn't have the ability to think that thought.

I write down on paper the same exact situation—anger at my mother, for example, or disappointment with my partner—and imagine it without the thought that is the cause of that anger or disappointment. Who would I be without that thought? How would I feel toward myself and others without that thought/belief? How might I move through my day and interact with others without that thought/belief? Without fail, when I explore this question with complete honesty, I find more peace, and a deeper sense of contentment with myself and the world.

The question, "Who would I be without the thought?" allows me to notice how differently I feel when I hold the belief as opposed to how I would feel without it. I notice that the radical difference

I feel is not produced from changing the outside world but from simply changing my own beliefs/thoughts!

## A Sample Application
Let's take a sample of a painful belief through "The Four Questions":

Painful belief: "He doesn't love me."

Question 1: "Is it true?"

Answer: "Yes." (If you follow your "yes" with thoughts like "because he left. Why else would he have left me?" you are no longer doing The Work. When you enter justification or defense, The Work stops working. Just answer with a simple "yes" or "no.")

Question 2: "Can you absolutely know that it's true?"

Answer: "Yes."

Question 3: "How do you react, what happens, when you believe that thought?"

Answer: "I am hurt and very angry with him. I act in desperate ways, using guilt, and I even threaten him to try to get him to stay. I act despondent and depressed - I even consider suicide. I stop taking care of myself. I feel rage toward him. I think that he should have loved me enough to stay. I think he's a liar, and I punish him for rejecting me. I call him names and am rude to him and his friends. I accuse him of anything I can think of and I make derisive, scathing remarks about him to my friends. I refuse to cooperate with him in any way. I refuse to speak with him at all. I tell anyone who will listen about how badly he treated me. I feel like a total victim."

Question 4: "Who would you be without the thought 'He doesn't love me?'"

Answer: "Without the thought 'He doesn't love me,' I wouldn't take his leaving so personally. I wouldn't feel so hurt or resentful toward him. I would be more focused on understanding, rather than blaming, him. I wouldn't feel so unlovable, which would free me up to understand the situation better. Without that thought, I would be better able to trust that things are working out for me. I could realize the potential of finding someone who is better suited for me and be excited about that. I could be more relaxed around him and treat him better. I wouldn't blame him for my hurt feelings. I would be kinder to myself. Rather than spiraling into depression and despondency, I would take better care of myself and in that way love me more. If I didn't believe that he doesn't love me, I would be able to love him unconditionally. I would appreciate all his wonderful qualities. I would be able to wish him the best in his new life. I would be happy that he is doing what he knows to do. I wouldn't need him to love me so much—or even at all—because I have me!"

## Finding the Turnarounds

Once we've asked ourselves the four questions, we take the next step in The Work. Byron Katie calls this next step the turnarounds. Now that we have questioned the original statement, "He doesn't love me," as thoroughly as we can and seen the cause-and-effect of believing it and had a glimpse of who we would be without it, we turn it around to its opposite. There may be several opposites for our original belief.

Going back to our sample, we write, "He doesn't love me." Then, we write its opposite: "He does love me."

How could that statement be true in your life? How could it be true that he loves you, even though he left you? Find at least three specific, genuine examples of how that statement is true. Here are some possibilities:

1. I can't know another person's mind and heart. I can't know how he is feeling toward me at this very moment.
2. In the larger scheme of things, letting me go may have been the best thing for me as well as for him. Letting me go may have been an act of love, for all I know.

3. He respected me enough to be honest with me.
4. He sounded kind to me when he said goodbye. It seemed as if he didn't want to hurt me.

There are also other types of turnarounds. For instance, we can turn the same statement around by substituting "I" or "me" for the pronouns, "he" or "him." For example: "He doesn't love me," turned around becomes "I don't love me." Yes, I can see how I abandon myself whenever I think punishing thoughts about how unloved or unlovable I am. Is it possible that my misery is caused by thoughts of being unloved? Am I hurt more from his leaving or my perception of how he betrayed me by leaving?

Here is another way to turn around the thought "He doesn't love me": "I don't love him." This example of a turnaround might bring to light how unloving I've been. Perhaps I left him too! Perhaps I moved out of the relationship even before he did! Find at least three specific, genuine examples of how you have been acting in an unloving way towards him. This may be difficult when you are feeling angry and abandoned. But it is the greatest kindness to yourself, because it levels the field, and is a step toward true humility and peace of heart. For more detailed instructions on the four questions and turnarounds, visit www.thework.com, or read Katie's book, *Loving What Is.*

Turnarounds are a very important part in the *BCP*. When we turn a troubling belief around and find examples of how its opposite is true, we often discern less painful ways of interpreting life. Rather than maintaining a *victim consciousness*, we can see and *align* with *Source*. We perceive what previously seemed to be impossibly difficult situations through newly opened eyes. We see peace and acceptance where, moments before, we saw only strife and discord.

Turnarounds also help us recognize our external judgments as the *projections* that they are. When we turn a judgmental accusation around, for instance, we may be surprised to find that we have been treating the other person in much the same way that we accuse them of treating us. Our harsh judgment of them is actually a reflection of something within us that we have judged, denied and *projected* onto them.

For example, my client Tina shared with me her conversation earlier that day with friends at work about how angry she was with her ex-husband: "I told them about how he always tries to make me look bad," she said. "He always puts me down and tells others about how bad I am."

Tina was totally surprised at the truth she discovered about herself when she questioned her statements about her husband and then turned them around. Her accusations about him turned around became: "I always try to make my ex-husband look bad. I put him down and tell others about how bad he is." It was quickly apparent to Tina that she was doing the same exact thing she was accusing her ex-husband of doing! She was "trying to make him look bad" to her friends by "telling others about how bad he was!" And this wasn't just a general statement: she was able to find many specific instances of how and where and when she had done this. Our judgments and accusations of others, more often than not, are an apt description of the way we are treating them at that very moment!

Since judgment is, in truth, a finger pointing back at us to show us what we have condemned and/or not accepted about ourselves, and since it will therefore be something we continue to do as long as we hold any degree of self-condemnation, why not use it to learn everything we can? This is what Byron Katie recommends. She devised a "Judge-Your-Neighbor Worksheet," (http://www. thework.com/downloads/worksheets/JudgeYourNeighbor_031810. pdf ) which shows us how to put our negative judgments to work for us through the four questions and turnarounds of The Work.

We can use our negative judgments to help us find what we have not forgiven in ourselves. The saying "If you spot it, you got it!" is applicable here. When we find ourselves harshly judging another, we learn to turn our focus within, to look for that in us that we have judged, avoided, and denied. We look for the thought within our own mind that is judging us and locate the belief behind it. And then we question the belief, and turn it around.

## A Sample Application

To illustrate what can happen when we practice using turnarounds, I'm including an example of a real life situation shared with me by Sue about her own *BCP* around her break-up with her boyfriend. As you will see, she was able to see the potentially excruciating situation in a way that dramatically reduced her experience of pain. The perspective she shares here is an example of what's possible when we question our thoughts and opt for *higher frequency* thinking. Here is my paraphrase of what Sue reported to me one week after her boyfriend of seven years broke up with her.

> *Jerry ended our relationship over the weekend. I was impressed by his honesty. Our conversation was surprisingly amicable, even loving. He told me he needed to break up with me. He said he was convinced it was the right thing to do - that he could see we needed to separate because we had grown apart.*
>
> *Although, at first I felt defensive, I decided to practice what I've been learning and so I tried to listen to him without personalizing what he said. I quickly realized I had a choice: I could choose to react painfully to what he was saying or I could choose to trust that I would be okay whatever happened. I chose to trust and that attitude made all the difference in how things turned out.*
>
> *I was able, as a result, to appreciate him for telling me his truth, and told him so. Jerry admitted that he had been unhappy with me for a while because of things that had happened between us in the past. He told me he had developed feelings for another woman, someone he worked with. He felt they had more in common than we had. He said he did not want to cheat on me and so he felt the need to be honest with me about his feelings for the other woman.*
>
> *I am glad he told me the truth. I can see how much more painful it might have been for me if I had found out about the situation from someone else. He appeared genuinely concerned for my feelings and that helped. Thinking about it,*

*I feel relieved that Jerry did not decide to stay out of guilt or pity, which might have turned to resentment and bitterness and perhaps prevented us both from finding someone better suited for us. As painful and scary as it is to move on, I have to agree with him that letting go of our unhappy relationship is the best, and most loving thing to do.*

Although Sue felt sad, she also felt a great deal of relief, and yes, even excitement, about her future.

Notice the *high-frequency* feelings that are generated by Sue's words as opposed to the *low-frequency* feelings generated by her *core belief*, "He doesn't love me because he left me." It should be obvious that Sue's response leads to gentler, kinder treatment, not only of her ex-boyfriend, but also of herself. The way Sue handled the break-up makes a continuing friendship possible with her ex. It may even be that they find themselves able to appreciate and support each other in ways they could not have previously imagined.

Unfortunately, most of us don't perceive the world with kindness. A significant shift in perception is required before we can see our daily situations with loving kindness as Sue was able to do in her breakup with Jerry. Her words illustrate a secret to inner peace: forgiving others is the kindest, most loving thing we can do for ourselves. When we question our limiting thoughts/beliefs we, in essence, shift our *emotional frequency* to a higher *vibration*, a *vibration* more compatible with our best selves, one that affirms our life experience and helps us view all of our relationships with love.

Using methods such as The Work of Byron Katie in our *BCP* is a fast, effective way to adjust our thinking to a *higher frequency* and return to inner peace. For that reason, I recommend memorizing Katie's four questions in the exact words that I have given above. We learn to use them, along with the turnarounds, as part of our everyday interaction. By practicing The Work in little situations that arise in our day-to-day life, we are more likely to remember to apply them when we are in severe emotional distress. The more we practice, the more effective we become at locating the negative thought causing our unhappiness, questioning it, and turning it around.

## *Planting a Seed of Doubt*

By questioning our negative thoughts and turning them around we essentially step back from them which allows us to see them differently. This stepping back through a questioning process is key to dismantling *core beliefs* because it allows us to plant a seed of doubt about the negative belief that is dominating our thoughts. We plant a seed of doubt by stepping back into our *observer consciousness* to reflect on our beliefs/thoughts and to question them, as Sue did when she refused to personalize Jerry's decision to leave their relationship. When we insert reasonable doubt between us and an unhappy thought, we free ourselves from having to act as if that thought is true. This allows a totally different outcome.

When we believe our thoughts, we become them. That means our thoughts and feelings arise out of the thoughts we believe. We become one with our beliefs. When we marry our thoughts, we automatically feel and act as if what we believe is true. The Work allows us to step back and *observe* our beliefs, question them, and then turn them around; in that way we detach from, or divorce, our troublesome thoughts. In other words, we move from a *reactive* mindset: a state of consciousness that perceives the world through a limited, unhappy viewpoint, into a reflective mindset.

From a reflective mindset, i.e. *observer consciousness*, we quiet the impulse to *react* in negative ways that verify our troubling beliefs. *Observing* and questioning, rather than *reacting*, is the key to achieving happier outcomes in all our day-to-day situations. By stepping back into *observer consciousness* we make room for other, more positive, possibilities to emerge.

CHAPTER EIGHT

# BCP Method 3:
# Body Awareness Methods

Healing our minds so that we lapse less often into *victim con-sciousness* awakens our true spiritual nature. To free our-selves from *victim consciousness*, we must *clear* and *align* our whole self: mentally, emotionally, and physically. Although the body is generally the last aspect of *consciousness* we pay attention to, it is nonetheless a vital part of our spiritual awakening, and therefore tending body issues is essential in the process of freeing ourselves from *victim consciousness*.

The third method for *clearing* negative beliefs uses the physi-cal body as an integral part of the process. Using *body awareness methods* we learn to recognize and use the body as a mirror that reflects to us our present state of relationship with ourselves.

The physical body manifests our internalized beliefs through our mannerisms and habitual postures. Through such physical expression we transmit the energy field of our early childhood and of our wounded child/self, that part of us that sees ourselves as somehow damaged. In other words, painful beliefs are not only carried in our minds, they are stored in our very cells. Our *core beliefs* literally shape our physical body and create an energy field that transmits *victim* energy and attracts to us more of the same.

In other words, our own *victim consciousness* manifests through us in a definite physical form that is tailor-made to exude the ambience of the *core beliefs* that define us and reinforce our expectations for life. This so called, "*victim posture*" is made up of long-standing physical habits, otherwise known as physical *defenses*. The child's wounded posture, skillfully covered, perhaps by a thin veneer of confidence skillfully hides our wounded concept of ourselves from the world.

The body is the most obvious, and yet perhaps the most overlooked, place we look to for help to free ourselves from *victim consciousness*. We have grown up in a world that thinks of the body as being irrelevant to our emotional well-being. In truth, however, the body has much to reflect and teach us about ourselves. The body holds the key to essential truths, not only in understanding ourselves better, but also in releasing ourselves from painful energetic patterns that hold us captive in *victim consciousness*.

Applying *body awareness methods* to *align* and *clear* our body of the painful beliefs that keep it bound in patterns of physical pain is not only possible, but it is a highly effective way to free ourselves from *victim consciousness*. Understanding the relevance our body has to our emotional health comes from understanding how our beliefs literally shape and energize or de-energize our physical body.

*Body awareness* simply means we bring *observer consciousness* into our relationship with our physical body. We begin to apply the same techniques to our body that we used to explore and release our limiting mental concepts; we learn to use the body as an experiential laboratory where we test and verify the *guiding principles* we established in the beginning of this book. The goal is to bring our physical body, along with our mental and emotional body, into the highest *alignment* possible with *Source*.

Having come to understand that it is the emotional residue from our *core beliefs* that holds our particular *victim posture* in place and inhibits our movement, we learn to use our body's signals as pointers to freedom. Through our habits of posture, our mannerisms, and where we experience pain (chronic pain is often related to the way we think and believe), we can locate and *clear* underlying *core beliefs* in and through the physical body.

## Identifying Core Beliefs in Physical Posture

Many of us have habits of poor posture of some sort. Those habits reflect painful beliefs that are stored in the body. Have we ever stopped to consider that our habitual body slouch or shoulder slump may be the result of our limiting beliefs? For instance, if we think we are unworthy, how might our posture reflect that belief? I visualize slumped shoulders and head. Habits of poor posture caused by limiting thoughts/beliefs eventually lead to physical pain and even structural problems in the body. In other words, physical pain is often the result of old, limiting beliefs that we carry in our cells.

Let's use an imaginary figure - we'll call him Davis - who operates from a belief that the world is dangerous. He constantly looks for evidence of danger. He suspects everyone he knows as having ulterior or dangerous motives. Davis is ever ready to be attacked from some unexpected place. Can we visualize the body posture such a belief might instigate?

Here's how I visualize Davis in my own mind: I see him, as he walks, with a tendency to slink forward rather than to stride forward with confidence. I see him slouching and furtively looking around when he stands, always on the lookout for danger. In my mind's eye, he fiddles nervously when he speaks, and I see how quickly he becomes startled at the least unexpected thing.

Now imagine that Davis has held these beliefs of the world as a dangerous place for a long time, maybe ten, twenty, even thirty years. What started out to be occasional paranoia has now become habitual. His physical mannerisms revolve around his fear-based beliefs and he has established a physical pattern that mirrors the anxiety, resentment, and distrust he regularly feels. This uncomfortable pattern has become his body's status quo; it's the way Davis moves through life. His pattern of beliefs has taken over his body and mind. These fearful beliefs have established a *victim mindset* that keeps him locked into a painful physical pattern that, in turn, reinforces his painful mindset. The mind and body are now working together to keep him in *victim consciousness*.

What's just as interesting is that the body pattern Davis has acquired causes him to look and act the part of a *victim*. In the same way a wounded bird alerts his predator by floundering about, Davis exudes *victim consciousness* through his physical patterns, and so attracts to himself those persons who will reinforce his beliefs about the world. In other words, his body language invites others to take advantage of him, to *victimize* him. Rather than protecting him from a dangerous world, his physical posturing instead attracts the danger he expects.

Of course Davis is unaware that he is sending out physical messages that reinforce his beliefs about the world. Instead he continues to foster those beliefs which cause his body to contract in painful patterns of fear and paranoia and thus perpetuate an ongoing *victim consciousness.*

Davis' acquired body pattern is by no means an unusual or rare occurrence. We all have body patterns that correlate to *core beliefs* and shape our life experience. All we have to do is look around and *observe* them.

For instance, we can detect depression in the way a person moves. They may walk with their head down, or their shoulders slumped. Another person unconsciously clenches their fists and habitually storms around; their body energy indicates anger. All of us have an emotional history that we transmit physically to the world around us, creating an *emotional frequency* that attracts to us the people and circumstances that end up verifying that history. It is worthwhile to begin to pay attention to how our bodies carry our *core beliefs.* By paying attention to such body language cues as noticing our physical posture, our mannerisms, etc, we can begin to make conscious the unhappy *core beliefs* that determine our state of *consciousness.*

We are beginning to see how our bodies reflect our *core beliefs.* Our task is to find the beliefs underneath the physical pain. We learn to do so in much the same way we link emotional pain to its related *core belief.*

I often tell my clients that everything we have ever experienced is stored in the cells of our body. I have spent years studying ways to access our body's stored trauma and also studying how to clear that trauma. Using *body awareness methods* we can indeed do just that; we can access the trauma and *clear* ourselves of the negative beliefs we are carrying, and in that way, we can free the mind of limitation and heal the body as well.

## Liberating the Mind through the Body

**An Example:**
In his session with me, Terry was exploring the childhood origins of his deep-seated, negative *core belief* that he was unimportant. I asked him to share with me his earliest memory that related to that belief. With eyes closed, he promptly began to recall times in his childhood when his father had ignored or rebuffed him.

I asked him to visualize his posture as that little boy who had been rebuffed, and then asked him to model it for me now. He stood up, dropped his gaze to the floor, slumped his shoulders and crossed his arms in what appeared to be a tightly contracted attempt to protect his heart. I asked Terry to say out loud the painful thoughts that accompanied his *victim posture*. With downcast eyes, he said, "I don't matter." Terry had just found the physical embodiment of his *victim pattern*.

Over the next few minutes, Terry and I explored together how his physical *victim pattern* transmitted the limiting energy of his *core belief*, "I don't matter," and how that belief held in his posture actually attracted to him the sort of responses from others that would verify that belief. Terry noticed that the places in his body that were most affected by his *victim pattern* were the places where he routinely experienced the most physical discomfort. In other words, wherever his *victim pattern* pulled him out of *physical alignment* were the places he experienced chronic aches and pain.

We began to apply "The Four Questions and Turn Arounds" to his thoughts of worthlessness as Terry began to seek a better standing *alignment*. As he stood in better *physical alignment*, I asked him to turn the belief, "I don't matter" around and feel the difference energetically.

"I matter" he said and began to recite examples to substantiate that thought. "I matter because I am alive," he said. "I matter to me ... to others ... to God. I matter." As he spoke he continued to straighten and *align* until he stood before me in his best posture yet, his face alight with a sincere smile.

At his next visit, Terry told me he was becoming increasingly aware of when he was out of *alignment*, lapsing back into his *victim pattern*, - and he said he was better able to bring himself back into *alignment*, both physically and mentally/emotionally as a result. His experience is one example of a way to use *body awareness* to liberate ourselves from *victim consciousness*.

Next I want to share with you an example taken from my own personal experience with a b*ody awareness method*. It illustrates how accessing and *clearing* can be accomplished using visualization and *physical alignment* through the practice of yoga and/or some type of energy work such as *qigong*.

**From My Journal: A Morning Practice**

*This morning I was practicing qigong. While moving my hands in slow, fluid motion, I became aware of the palpable difference in energy between various areas of my mid-body. Without physically touching my body, I suddenly noticed how different the energy felt on the right front side of my body in contrast to the left front side.*

*The energy on the right side felt thick, heavy, and cloying as opposed to a light feeling on the left side. I began to make motions with my hands as if I were pulling the dark, cloying energy out of the right side. Using intention and imagination, I visualized my hands pulling the dark energy up and out.*

*As I continued to work towards balancing my energy, I began to hear specific thoughts run through my mind. A belief began to emerge as I worked with the thick darkness. It was a belief about being sick. I could actually feel the accumulated cloying heaviness of that deep-seated belief I'd been carrying for some time that said, "I am sick and cannot get well."*

*As I continued to silently move my hands, intentionally mixing and balancing the energy throughout my body, my observer consciousness moved forward to calmly and gently* meet the belief. Rather than judge the thoughts, I simply began to question their accuracy.

"Is that true?" "Do I absolutely know that I cannot get well?" "Who am I when I believe that thought?" "How does that belief affect the way I see myself and the world?" These are the questions I asked myself as I continued to balance my body energy. More related thoughts rose to the surface.

I noticed how one thought seemed to give birth to another thought of the same energy frequency. The thoughts congregated around that central, or core belief, "I'm sick and can't get well" until I felt mentally glutted with thoughts of that same energy frequency. I could see how I had come to see myself through that limited mindset.

I heard thoughts like, "It's inevitable; it's only a matter of time before I get really sick again," and, "I don't deserve to be well. I'm being punished for all the poor choices I've made in the past," followed by, "I'm too old. Old bodies cannot stay well. My body is not strong enough; it's too late; I've waited too long to do anything about my health." Such negative thoughts streamed through my mind and I did not try to stop them. I just stayed physically aligned and continued to move through my qigong practice, breathing in a slow, deep rhythm while observing and questioning my thoughts.
I asked myself:

"Do I absolutely know that any of these thoughts are true?" I questioned the thoughts one by one, As I explored my thoughts about my body, I focused on energetically balancing it. I asked myself "What would it be like to be free of such limiting thoughts?" I could feel the heaviness begin to dissipate as I envisioned the freedom and lightness of believing the exact opposite of those thoughts now fading.

The heaviness continued to dissipate until finally, the dark, cloying energy on the right side had completely gone. I could suddenly breathe more deeply than before. I envisioned light inside me and my body indeed felt lighter, more vibrant and relaxed.

The above account is an example using a *body awareness method* as a part of the *daily practice*. The contrast between the way I felt in the beginning of that morning's practice and the way I felt at the end seems miraculous in hindsight. By showing up everyday and *aligning* with *Source*, we begin to open a dialog between the physical body and our intuitive self that is capable of teaching, prompting, and healing us. I continue to use *body awareness methods* like those described above as an essential part of my own *daily practice*.

## Seeing the Body as a Mirror

Our body, like the external world, is a reflection of our mind. The physical form mirrors our beliefs. Our posture, facial expressions, physical habits, and gestures all reflect and transmit our beliefs for the world to see.

If we distrust life and see the world as scary, our posture and physical *reaction* to life will model those beliefs. If we believe the world is unfair or unjust, our movement will mirror that world view. We might drop our heads and cast our eyes downward when we walk as a way of attempting to fly beneath the radar of a hostile world. Or, we might twist our mouths in a perpetual frown and hunch our shoulders, signaling how burdened we feel by the world. As Terry's example indicated, we all have a physical *victim pattern* that transmits the *vibrational frequency* of our *core beliefs*.

This idea of transmitting thoughts physically may explain why animals respond the way they do to people. Many dogs, for instance, are masters at reading a person's *intentions* from physical body cues. They pick up right away on a person's *vibrational frequency*. Our bodies constantly transmit the *emotional frequency* and the nature of our thoughts.

For example: I have a family member who believes life is against him. I know this not only by the things he says, but also by the way he walks. He marches heavily and tends to bump into things as he moves across a room. He unconsciously slams cabinet doors and moves with an air of determined impatience. It's as if he is *resisting* life, fighting against it, with every step he takes. His body gives him away. It transmits his beliefs.

We all know someone whose posture exudes anger, depression or fear; what we see in their physical presentation is the physical manifestation of their negative beliefs. We too, physically transmit our beliefs.

As long as we continue to shape our bodies with negative thoughts/beliefs, there will be pain. When our bodies are out of correct *physical alignment*, when we replace good posture with habitual patterns of *defense* because we believe our painful thoughts, we create for ourselves physical discomfort, tension, aches/pains, and eventually disease. In other words, our *core beliefs* can incapacitate us. They keep us from giving and receiving love; they keep us from being able to move through life physically free of pain and limitation. They keep us from inner peace. By integrating the *BCP* into our *daily practice*, we begin to free our mind and our body from the thoughts/beliefs that hold us prisoner, mentally and physically.

Through various body modalities such as yoga and *qigong*, we learn the importance of being *physically aligned*. Proper *physical alignment* is imperative for optimum performance and we learn to pay a lot of attention to it during our practice. We strive to perfect our *physical alignment* by making subtle physical shifts and changes, often with the help of a mirror, so we can achieve best results. We acquire a feel for when we are in good *physical alignment* and when we are out of *alignment*. We notice that when we are in proper *physical alignment* we are less prone to muscle soreness and injury.

The same principles that apply to *physical alignment* apply to our internal and emotional *alignment* too. We practice optimum *alignment* not only in the body, but also in *aligning* our minds with *Source*. When we come into true *alignment* with *Source* we experience tremendous benefits. For instance, *alignment* with *Source* allows us to be at peace regardless of the outer circumstances of our life. When we are *aligned*, we see the same things we saw before we found peace, but we interpret them very differently.

*Aligned*, we perceive the universe as a friendly, supportive place, rather than as a dangerous place where we cannot express ourselves or live our lives creatively and freely.

When we are in *alignment* with *Source*, we expect something good to come from whatever happens. Rather than *reacting* out of fear (a chief characteristic of *victim consciousness*) we see life challenges as part of the design to expand us.

Instead of perceiving the world as mean or unfair, we come to see it literally, as a mirror for us of both the personal and collective mind. Such a shift in perception comes from practicing daily *alignment*. Rather than moving through our day with a sense of foreboding, we find ourselves able to meet life events with a sense of curiosity and openness.

In *alignment* we trust things to be the way they need to be, whether we understand or not why things are the way they are. In *alignment* with *Source* and *Reality* we no longer focus on problems; instead we focus on what is working. We develop a practice of wanting what we have because we understand that there are no mistakes or coincidences; we understand that everything we experience is tailor made to move us towards deeper self-realization.

The practice of *emotional* and *physical alignment* with *Source* does not mean that we give up in defeat or settle for something less than desirable; it means we settle more deeply into a habitual, loving relationship with *Reality*. Instead of automatically *reacting* from *victim consciousness,* we stop and consciously *align* with *Reality*. In so doing we restore peace. To *align* with *Source* daily helps us accept, even embrace, the circumstances of our lives. We respond from a state of mental clarity, and we are no longer slaves to our old limiting beliefs.

# CHAPTER NINE

# Victim Consciousness

## Summary

*Victim consciousness* results from a lifetime habit of thinking like a *victim* or living in a state of *victim consciousness*. *Victim consciousness* predominates in today's world and causes us to see ourselves, and others, in sorely limited ways. It is our own thoughts/beliefs that produce *victim consciousness* and not the circumstances of our lives. Our own negative thoughts/beliefs are the sole cause of our unhappiness.

*Victim consciousness* is not about the things that happen to us, it is about the way we choose to perceive what is happening to us. It is a mental condition that prompts us to see ourselves as mistreated, unfortunate, unlucky, and at the mercy of an unfair world.

We are in *victim consciousness* whenever we are in any of the three roles (*persecutor, rescuer,* or *victim*) on the *victim triangle*. All the roles operate from *victim consciousness* and therefore perpetuate the belief that we are *victims*.

In *victim consciousness* we think our misery/unhappiness is caused by our conditions and life circumstances. We think we have no choice except to feel bad when "bad" things happen. We think our external conditions have to dictate our level of peace and happiness. None of these ideas is true even though they are widespread and commonly believed. Such are the myths we hope we have helped to dispel through the information presented in these pages.

It is never our external situation, nor the people in our lives, that determine our state of happiness, or *victim* status. Jewish psychiatrist and concentration camp survivor, Viktor Frankl, said it well in his acclaimed book, <u>Man's Search For Meaning</u> (1959), which is his own story of survival: "... even the helpless victim of a hopeless situation (like living in a concentration camp), facing a fate he cannot change, may rise above himself. He may turn a personal tragedy into a triumph"(p. 146).

Frankl said basically the same thing we have been discovering here; he found that it was not the external conditions that determined his camp mates' state of mind, but their attitude toward those conditions. We either see ourselves at the mercy of external conditions and therefore as *victims*, or we see an opportunity to raise our *consciousness*.

By applying the ideas and principles presented here we may come to discredit the idea that there is any such thing as a real *victim*. To state such an opinion does not mean that we deny or ignore the horrible things that happen in the world; yes, there is rape, murder, and war. Unfortunately many of us endure these things. But these life circumstances do not determine whether or not we behave like *victims*. Only when we believe and perceive ourselves as *victims*, are we doomed to live as *victims*. Only if we believe ourselves to be at the mercy of hardship and the life challenges we go through, are we defined by hardships and life challenges. It is possible to go through horrendous life circumstances and remain mentally and emotionally free. Our life events alone cannot define us; we are not *victims*, ever, unless we ourselves agree to being *victims*. Through the tools we present here, we learn to liberate ourselves from *victim consciousness* from the inside out so that we may live our lives free of any vestige of it.

When we meet our thoughts with the curiosity of an inquiring mind, rather than meeting them with judgment and attempts to silence them, our thoughts can lead us to the peace that only comes from *aligning* with *Reality*. Our judgments about others are especially instructive because they work like fingers pointing our attention to the "culprit thought" within us that is truly disturbing our peace. We meet our troubling thoughts, one by one, and we ask them what their business is with us so we can decide if we want to partner with them or not.

We get to choose whether or not we want to entertain the thoughts we think and the healthiest criteria upon which to base that choice is the *emotional frequency* they produce in us - *low-frequency* or *high-frequency*? If our thought produces angst, unhappiness, or fear, we learn to explore its opposite to see if there's reason to believe the reverse thought might be at least as true. The thoughts we choose to believe rule not only in that moment, they rule the outcomes of our lives.

When we consistently believe *low-frequency* thoughts we spend our days on the *victim triangle* in most, if not all, of our relationships. To free ourselves from *victim consciousness* we must move into *observer consciousness*. Doing so allows us to turn our *low-frequency* thought into a *higher frequency* thought. The *victim triangle* is thus flipped right side up into a positive and empowering *triangle of health and well-being*.

We transform the *victim* roles we've been addicted to playing (*rescuer, persecutor, victim*) into their higher functioning roles, (*nurturer, asserter, observer*). This means that rather than *rescue* and/or attack, we learn to empower others. Rather than feel at the mercy of the world outside of us, we see our choices and consciously opt to *align* with *Reality* and *Source*.

The key is to practice in all of our affairs the *guiding principles* (pp. 3 & 4) outlined in the beginning of this book. Through our *daily practice we* begin to follow the three directives elucidated in Part II, Chapter 1: we *show up,* we *align,* and we *clear* (pp. 53-57) our minds and our body.

By making those three directives a regular part of our *daily practice* we develop a healing relationship between our highest best self and *Source* that allows us to carry the *guiding principles* into our life experience, debunk *victim consciousness,* and move into a higher state of *consciousness* instead,

*Aligning* with *Source* is the key. Remember, *Source* is the emanating light and energy that sustains and animates us. What we do with that sustaining energy is up to us, but we know that the light of *Source*, because it is light, illuminates darkness. What that means is that *Source*, as light, shines on our false beliefs and makes them visible. Through the intervention of *Source* we realize our best selves and encounter people and situations that help us see ourselves, and life in general, more clearly. In other words, *Source* shines the light of truth on our lives so that *Reality* is revealed. As a result we are able to dismiss the untruths and painful beliefs that have kept us living limited lives. *Source* shows us beliefs in action so we can choose something more desirable for ourselves.

*Observer consciousness,* the antidote to *victim consciousness,* is our own internal emissary. It is the inner voice that directly communes with and connects us to *Source.* Even though we are born with access to *observer consciousness,* in many of us it is sorely underdeveloped from lack of use. Developing our *observer consciousness* by committing to a *daily practice is* the most effective way to hasten our release from *victim consciousness.*

Tapping into *observer consciousness,* regardless of the external circumstances, allows us to disengage from our painful beliefs and explore the impact upon us of believing them. It is an absolute requirement for stepping out of *victim consciousness.*

Through the act of *observing,* we notice repetitive patterns of thought that appear to relate to a central theme, or *core belief.* Getting to know our own *core beliefs* and the painful and endless cycle they perpetuate (see the step by step process outlined on pp. 95-112) is another step in freeing ourselves from the *victim consciousness.* Once we know our *core beliefs* we learn to look for them instead of automatically acting in accord with them.

The tools of inquiry that include "The Four Questions and Turn Arounds" (Katie and Mitchell, 2002) are ideal as a quick way to access our *observer consciousness* and provide a way to investigate and detach from the *core beliefs* and negative thoughts that otherwise completely control our feelings and behavior. Through tools like "The Four Questions and Turn Arounds" we can free our minds from *victim consciousness.*

Healing for the body is also possible. Through resources like the *body awareness methods* we can apply *observer consciousness* to the physical body and free it from painful *victim patterns* and unhealthy postures that we've accumulated.

Freedom from *victim consciousness* entails operating out of an awakened state of *consciousness*, the *observer consciousness*, that allows us to shift our focus from the external world as the cause of our unhappiness to our internal world as the cause. We learn to *align* all three bodies, mental, emotional and physical, with *Source* and *Reality* by applying the *guiding principles* explored here in a daily lifestyle that engenders peace and acceptance of self and others. True freedom from *victim consciousness* is attained daily, thought by thought. It is something we can choose to give ourselves in any moment by detaching from the thoughts and beliefs that cause our pain. We are free the moment we plant a seed of doubt between ourselves and our next limiting thought.

It is important for us to remember that we are more than our biological, psychological, and sociological conditions. We are more than our heredity and environment. To think that these things define and determine us is to see ourselves as *victims* to our outer influences and inner conditions. Yes, to be sure, we all must live within certain limitations that we are powerless over. There are disabilities and a lack of certain abilities we all have that cannot be changed, but these do not make us *victims*. It is not our external conditions and situations that determine our freedom from *victim consciousness*, it is our internal attitude towards these limitations that determine our inner freedom.

We are self-determining. We have the ultimate right and power to decide what the quality of our life will be. We practice that right by choosing what to believe about our conditions and life situations. In other words, it's the attitude we choose to have towards what happens to us that determines the quality of our life experience. That choice, not our life circumstances, decides whether we will live a life full of meaning and purpose, or whether we will go on living our lives in the throes of a misery-making *victim consciousness*. May we rise above our conditions, elevate our thoughts by reframing the beliefs that cause us pain and by so doing, find the inner peace and connection with *Source* that results.

# Glossary

**alignment, align, aligning:** the act of setting ones intention to the purpose of coming into direct connection with *Source* for the purpose of achieving inner peace and healing.

**alignment process:** *clearing* stressful thoughts and opening energy channels in the mind and body so that we can be present to receive the healing, guidance, and direction constantly available from *Source*.

**asserter:** a role on the *triangle of health and well-being* that is the transformed version of the *persecutor* on the *victim triangle*. The *asserter* is able to set aside *defenses* and respond with calm strength, firmness, clarity, and kindness that can only come from someone who has given up the need to be right and truly expects a peaceful and sane response from others.

**authentic self, authenticity:** the essential essence we are each born with; that aspect of us that is real, eternal, and indestructible as separate from the mind-made self (consisting of our ideas/beliefs about ourselves) we more often identify with.

**belief clearing process (BCP):** used to dismantle negative *core beliefs* using various and specific methods described in this book, all of which encourage us to assume responsibility for our own *low-frequency* beliefs and to reframe them.

**body awareness method:** using yoga and *qigong* or similar energy-based practices for the purpose of clearing the physical *victim patterns* we carry in our body; using visualization and various postures and movements to find the negative *core beliefs* we carry in the body and, through aligning, releasing them.

***boundaries:*** establishing limits so that we are consciously aware and respectful of the rights of oneself and others. To recognize and respect the differences between our own ideas, needs, thoughts, and feelings and those of others. To maintain a clear sense of what we are responsible for, and what we are not responsible for, and to respond from that awareness.

***bubble of protection:*** a way of praying for safety that envisions a bubble surrounding the people and possessions we are concerned about, and in that way creating a *high-frequency* energy field of belief in protection.

***clear, cleared, clearing, clearing process:*** methods used to clear the negative beliefs that separate us from *Reality*; to free our mind from stressful, unhealthy thoughts and *core beliefs*, to bring us back into *alignment* with *Source*.

***consciousness:*** our state (negative or positive) of mental awareness, or our degree of wakefulness towards *Reality*.

***core belief cycle (CBC):*** a repetitive cycle involving the enactment of a negative life theme that usually originates in childhood from *negative life decisions* we made based on our limited interpretation of childhood events, family messages, and *unmet needs*.

***core beliefs:*** a particular set of *low-frequency* beliefs we adopt, usually in childhood, that limit our ability to see and experience a positive life of joy and acceptance. *Core beliefs* arise from our original wounding experiences and consist of our explanations for how and why those things happened. A *core belief* is an unquestioned assumption about who we are or what the world is like; *core beliefs* are often unconsciously formed before we learn to speak.

***daily practice:*** a method or daily discipline to *align* with *Source* for the purpose of *clearing* and healing the mind and body so that we can better express our highest, best self. It can include any form of meditation or movement that helps us *align* our *intention* with the *high-frequency* of *Source*.

***defenses, defensively, defensive, defended, defending, defensive reactions:*** creative, but mostly dysfunctional, ways of acting, medicating, denying, *projecting,* and/or avoiding painful feelings so to escape their impact. *Defenses* are the behaviors, addictions, and activities we engage in for the purpose of stuffing, denying, or medicating uncomfortable and unresolved feelings.

***emotional alignment:*** process of *clearing* our distorted thinking and core beliefs for the purpose of attaining a state of peace and well-being that is congruent and directly linked to *Source*.

***emotional frequency:*** a term used to refer to the vibrational high or low quality of a feeling state. We refer to two *frequency* states to which all feelings belong: feelings are either *high-frequency* or they are *low-frequency. Low-frequency* feelings cause a state of internal contraction and lead to *resistant reactions*; they include feelings such as fear, resentment, discouragement, depression, guilt, doubt, etc. *High-frequency* feelings elevate our mood and disposition and include feelings such as gratitude, acceptance, joy, caring, harmony, centered relaxation, etc.

***emotional charge:*** an unresolved, often unconscious, set of feelings carried over from a painful childhood event. Because there was no frame of reference or understanding provided at the time of origination, *clearing* was not possible, and the unprocessed emotion is stored in the unconscious. When something in the present triggers the unprocessed memory, the emotional charge is re-experienced causing us to *react defensively* as if the thing were happening all over again.

**externally oriented perception:** (See *internally oriented perception*) a perception based on the belief that ones well-being is determined by and dependent upon outside events beyond our control. A *victim's* perception: *victim consciousness*.

**"Faces of Victim":** the title of an article I wrote that details the roles of *victim* as originally described by Stephen Karpman, phd. The "Faces" are the three roles found on the Drama Triangle: *persecutor, rescuer,* and *victim.*

**Four Questions and Turn Arounds:** a process of inquiry developed by Byron Katie, (http://www.thework.com/index.php) designed to help us recognize and release stressful thoughts. These four straight-forward questions and their turn arounds, when explored truthfully, have the ability to restore our emotional balance and return us to peace.

**frequency:** a level of *vibration.*

**frequency adjustment:** a process by which we raise our mental and/ or emotional *vibrational frequency* to a higher level to facilitate our sense of well-being.

**frequency path:** the *vibrational* path on which one is currently trav-eling as determined by the quality of one's thoughts and feelings and which determines the *emotional frequency* of the people and situa-tions we attract into our lives. If we are addicted to negative, stressful thoughts we are on a *low-frequency* path and will most likely expe-rience *low-frequency* results. When we *clear* our *low-frequency core beliefs* and practice *high-frequency* thoughts that generate acceptance, peace, and gratitude, we attract to ourselves *high-frequency* results.

**guiding principles:** a set of governing spiritual principles that we adopt and consciously cultivate in our daily lives to replace the *low-frequency* beliefs that have keep us so long trapped in *victim consciousness.*

**high(er,est) frequency:** thoughts, feelings, events, etc. that are positive and based on spiritual *guiding principles*, that are *aligned* with *Reality*, and that create a sense of peace and well-being. When we accept life on its own terms with an attitude of gratitude, we generate a *high-frequency* that will attract more of the same.

**intention, intend, intentional, intending:** the act of setting our mind towards achieving a particular goal, or to *align* ourselves mentally with a positive goal or direction of our choosing. To set our *intention* implies a positive, conscious directing of our personal will or desire. It is a powerful act precisely because it directs *qi*/universal energy. Practicing positive *intention* restores health, rejuvenates the body, and liberates the mind.

**internally oriented perception:** (see *externally oriented perception*) seeing life as being determined by our own mental thoughts and beliefs. To recognize that we, not outside factors, are responsible for the way we feel. The absence of blaming other people and external circumstances for our well-being.

**lineage beliefs:** *core beliefs* that come down to us from previous generations; family beliefs we adopt as our own but that did not originate out of our personal life experience. Such *core beliefs* can be difficult to recognize because we have never thought to question them, instead we simply live them out, failing to notice their *low-frequency* impact upon us.

**low(er) frequency:** thoughts, feelings, and ways of interacting that produce contraction, *resistance*, and negativity. *Low-frequency* feelings and thoughts are most often generated by distorted beliefs adopted in childhood that validate *victim consciousness*. *Low-frequency* feelings alert us that we are thinking unhappy thoughts and encourage us to investigate them.

**negative consequences:** the painful and negative cost, or price we pay, as a result of believing our limiting thoughts and *core beliefs*. Also see *payoffs*.

**negative family messages:** a term used on the *CBC* to denote messages sent verbally, non-verbally, and energetically to us as children by our significant caregivers and family members that we interpret as life-limiting, and from which we draw negative conclusions about ourself and the world around us.

**negative life decisions:** a term used to denote conclusions drawn by us from our interpretation of and interaction with family members; such decisions are often made unconsciously and at an early age, and include decisions about who we are and what we can expect from life.

**non-reactive:** to respond to life from a place of detached *observation*; a calm, centered emotional state that allows us to choose our behavioral responses, rather than to be ruled by old *core beliefs* and *defensive reactions*.

**NOW:** a term used by Eckhart Tolle to denote the present moment where it is possible to tap into *observer consciousness* and see *Reality* and connect with *Source*. The *NOW* is the only place where *Source* can be experienced because it is the only place that truly exists outside our mind-made illusion of time, past and future.

**nurturer:** one of three roles on the *triangle of health and well-being*, the *nurturer* is the *rescuer* transformed. Having discovered the difference between empowering others and enabling dependency, *nurturers* have moved away from believing that their worth comes from what they do for others and are instead able to support and nourish in ways that truly empower themselves and others.

**observer, observe, observing (see also *witness*):** the *victim* transformed. The *observer* is the aspect of ourself that *witnesses Reality* without the need to judge it harshly. The *observer* is our integrated self who operates from a set of *guiding principles* that allows it to respond to life from the *triangle of health and well-being,* rather than unconsciouslly *react* from one of the three roles on the *victim triangle (persecutor, rescuer, victim)*. Because it is *aligned* with *Source*, the *observer* operates from a *higher frequency* and therefore emanates a sense of non-*resistance* and peace.

**observer consciousness:** an in-born state of *consciousness* that sees the world through a set of basic *guiding principles* and generates in us a *higher emotional frequency. Observer consciousness* is the antidote to *victim consciousness.* From *observer consciousness* we are able to see *Reality* clearly and to respond appropriately to external stimuli. Rather than fearing the outside world, and in turn, blaming it for our problems, as *observers* we are compassionate *witnesses* of our life circumstances.

**observer triangle:** known as the *triangle of health and well-being,* the *observer triangle* is the transformed version of the *victim triangle,* drawn as an upright triangle with the three roles of *observer, nurturer,* and *asserter.*

**payoffs:** (also see *negative consequences):* the perceived benefit(s) that come from living out of our *defenses* and *persona*. Our conviction in these illusory *payoffs* prompt us to hold onto our *defenses* because we believe they serve us in some way. Until we make these *payoffs* conscious we will not be motivated to give up our *defenses,* no matter the *negative consequences* involved in keeping them.

**persecutor:** one of the three roles we move through on the *victim triangle* and a primary *starting gate position* that is often taken on by one who has been overtly mentally and/or physically abused during childhood. *Persecutors* tend to see themselves as *victims* of a dangerous world. They are constantly on the lookout for how they are being mistreated, tending to strike out against others they perceive as the enemy.

**persona:** a particular set of *defenses* we gather and wear as a mask or protective shield for the purpose of hiding our vulnerabilty. The *persona* is a mistaken or false identity made up of our *core beliefs* and protective *defenses* that affords us the illusion of safety in what otherwise feels to be an unsafe world. The *persona* is sometimes referred to as our personality.

**personal reality:** mind-made and limited perceptions of ourself, others, and the world which originate out of our own distorted convictions and *core beliefs*, and which we *project* onto the world around us and *react* out of. Our *personal reality* is made up of limited assumptions that we have never questioned, but simply presumed to be true. *Personal reality* lies in sharp contrast to the true *Reality* that is governed by a kind and loving *Source*. (See *Reality*.)

**physical alignment, physically align(ed):** our natural and best physical posture, which when achieved allows us to experience the greatest flow of *qi* or *Source* energy through the body. Through a *daily practice* of finding *physical alignment* we can *clear* the *victim pattern* created from our *core beliefs* and find relief from the painful *physical patterns* that throw us out of right *alignment* and that keep us disconnected from *Source*.

**practice:** see *daily practice*.

**projection, project, projecting, projected, projector:** the unconscious transfer of our opinions, judgments, *core beliefs*, desires and/or emotions onto the people and circumstances of our life. Once we transfer our own unconscious material onto others, we then tend to feel and act as if what we've transferred is true. We often then use the *projection* as evidence.

**qi:** the Chinese word for "energy." *Qi* is the life force that animates all life. It is the energy that comes directly from *Source*. The Chinese believe there are three types of *qi*: **1.** internal *qi*, the energy that fuels and maintains the whole physical system, including the organs, musculature, skeletal system, nervous system, and circulation. *Qi* is carried by the blood. Wherever there is poor circulation there is blocked *qi*; pain and disease follow. **2.** external *qi*, the life medium that surrounds us, what we call "air": as water is the supportive medium for fish, we are supported by a *qi*/energy field. **3.** miraculous *qi*, the living Intelligence of *Source* that hears and responds to us, and from which all miracles come.

***qigong*:** an ancient physical practice that originated in Eastern Asia and that uses breath, precise movement, and visualization to manipulate *qi*/energy for the purpose of healing. There are thousands of styles of *qigong*, each practiced for particular reasons, and includes all of the martial arts (karate, tai chi, aikido, tae kwon do, etc). The *qigong* referred to within this book is specifically practiced to facilitate physical and emotional healing.

***react, reactive, reacting, reaction(s), reactor*:** someone who is in a negative emotional state marked by *defensive* behavior towards a perceived threat. A *resistant* way of behaving when painful or limiting *core beliefs* are triggered by something someone says or does so that we act out of the automatic *defenses* that accompany *victim consciousness*.

***Reality* (see also *Source*):** the way things are right now, the "what-is" of this moment is *Reality*. *Reality* is *Source*-in-action. The job of *Reality* is to reflect our current inner state of *consciousness*. (See *personal reality*.)

***rescuer, rescue*:** one of the three roles that we move through on the *victim triangle*. *Starting gate rescuers* tend to believe that their total worth comes from what they do for others. *Rescuers* see their needs as unimportant and they tend to feel selfish when they take care of themselves. They are often self-sacrificing martyrs, controlling caretakers, and people-pleasers.

***resist(ed), resistance, resistant, resisting:*** anytime we struggle against, or deny *Reality* we are in *resistance*. *Resistance* is earmarked by *low-frequency* feelings such as resentment, guilt, fear, doubt, etc. and is generated when we think judgmental, negative thoughts. *Resistance* generally implies a tendency to strike out, fight against, or *resist* life mentally, verbally and/or physically.

***sanity:*** the stable emotional state that comes from being grounded in *Reality*. A non-*reactive*, rather than *reactive*, state of *consciousness*, free of painful assumptions and *core beliefs* about ourselves, others, and life. *Sanity* is the natural state of being that results from remembering who we truly are.

***show up, align, and clear:*** three directives to integrate into our lives on a daily basis for ultimum health and well-being.

***sincerity:*** an attitude of genuine belief cultivated in the *daily practice* that includes a sense of reverence and gratitude. When we practice with *sincerity* our connection with *Source* is much enhanced and the healing and beneficial results of our practice are greatly amplified.

***Source:*** the One Mind from which all things are created has been called by many names, including God, Yahweh, Great Spirit, etc; *Source* is the one true *Reality* that is always accepting, peaceful, and kind and that is alive, intelligent, and present in every moment. *Source* is capable of hearing and responding to us. It is the *highest frequency* possible. We can choose to *align* with *Source* and thus tap into Its protection and guidance.

***starting gate persecutor (SGP):*** views himself/herself as a *victim* in need of protection. P*ersecutors* justify their vengeful behavior, i.e. "I had to strike out to protect myself." He/she has a *core belief* that goes something like, "The world is dangerous, people can't be trusted so I need to get them before they hurt me." They inevitably blame and attack others.

***starting gate position:*** the habitual role of either *persecutor, victim, rescuer,* that we each have and from which we tend to start out from on the *victim triangle.* Each one of us has a *starting gate position* that we adopt early in life and each role has its own particular *core belief* that influences how it moves around the *victim triangle.* These *starting gate positions* become our primary way of seeing ourselves and are a strong part of our perceived identity.

***starting gate rescuer(SGR):*** views himself/herself as an ultra-responsible and capable helper, here to take care of others. *Rescuers* get their primary sense of worth from "saving" others and they often act in ways that encourage other people to be dependent on them. They unconsciously seek *victims* to *rescue* so they can feel needed, vital, and important.

***starting gate victim (SGV):*** views himself/herself as defective, weak, and lacking in what it takes to take care of themselves. *Victims* generally have *core beliefs* that promote a sense of "I can't." Because *victims* see themselves as incapable, inferior, and not smart, or not healthy enough to handle life adequately, they tend to constantly seek *rescuers* to take care of them.

***surrender, surrendering, surrendered:*** the act or process of letting go of the painful, limited thoughts, and *core beliefs* that create emotional angst in us and trust in the purposes and guidance of *Source:* ultimately to relax into total oneness with *Source.*

***triangle of health and well-being (see also victim triangle):*** the *higher frequency* version of the *victim triangle;* also called the *observer triangle.* Rather than pointing down like the *victim triangle* the *triangle of health and well-being* sits upright with the *observer* at the apex and the other two roles, *nurturer and asserter,* at the bottom corners: a triangle that represents the transformation of the three roles of the *victim triangle (persecutor, victim, rescuer).*

*triggered* (see *reactive*): the programmed, often automatic and negative emotional or behavioral *reaction* we experience when we are in
*victim consciousness*. *Low-frequency* feelings are *triggered* anytime
we believe we are at the mercy of outside events, or when we fail to
remember that our responses come from our own limiting thoughts
and *core beliefs* and not from what's happening outside us.

*unmet needs*: every human being has basic inborn physical, emotional,
mental, and spiritual needs that are vital to our well-functioning; for
instance, we all have needs for food, air, and shelter, as well as a need
for safety, belonging, validation, love, protection, security, stability,
etc. Born into families that, due to their own *unmet needs*, are not
able to meet such needs adequately, threatens our sense of self, and
prompts us to make *negative life decisions* that set us up for the *victim
triangle* and a painful *core belief cycle*.

*vibration, vibrating, vibrational, vibrational frequency*: a measuring
term used to determine the quality of lightness (as in "light as a feather")
as opposed to the quality of density or heaviness, (as in "heavy as a
crate of apples") of a particular thing. Our *vibrational frequency* is the
*high* or *low-frequency* quality of our thoughts, feelings (see *emotional
frequency*) and/or our state of being as determined by whether those
thoughts, feelings, or behavior come from a connection to the *higher
frequency* of *Source* (which generates love, acceptance, understanding)
or from a *lower frequency* source (which creates fear and/or *resistance*).

*victim(s), victimize*: a state of *consciousness* that prompts us to see
ourselves as being "done to by" or "at the mercy of" others. We fall
into *victim* whenever we do not take full responsibility for ourselves
(our thoughts, feelings, and behavior). We are in a *victim mind-set*
(see *victim consciousness*) anytime we believe that something (or
someone) outside us is the cause of our emotional well-being (either
our happiness or our unhappiness) we tend to react as a *victim*. Not
to be confused with being the recipient of an accident or crime; we
can experience trauma and not feel or see ourselves as *victims*.

**victim competition**: the tendency to gather evidence about how unfairly we have been treated and then use that evidence to convince another that we've been more mistreated than they have. We often see marriage partners engage in this sort of *victim competition*.

**victim consciousness**: we are in v*ictim consciousness* anytime we believe that our own inner state is caused by something outside of us. When we believe that other people, situations, and events are in control of our thoughts and feelings, or see ourselves as being at the mercy of an unkind world, we are in *victim consciousness*.

**victim ego**: the wounded part of us that see ourselves as being at the mercy of outside forces and is highly *defensive* and *reactive* as a result of maintaining a distorted perception based on *core beliefs* that perpetuate a painfully limited idea of who we are.

**victim energy field** (**see core belief cycle**): the *vibrational* energy field that is created when we *react* out of an assortment of *core beliefs* and painful *defenses*.

**victim mind, victim mentality** (**see victim or victim ego**): a learned and habitual style of relating that causes us to *react* from a place of fear or resentment, leaving us feeling trapped and/or without options.

**victim pattern, victim posture**: the physical pattern we carry in our bodies that corresponds to our painful *core beliefs*. *Victim consciousness* manifests in a definite physical posture that transmits the particular *victim mentality* we hold that reinforces *low-frequency* expectations in life.

**victim triangle** (**see reference for Karpman's Drama Triangle**): the playing field upon which our *core belief* dramas are played out. The *victim triangle* is a diagram of a downward facing triangle that shows the three roles (or *faces*) of *victim: persecutor, rescuer,* and *victim,* all of which have a tendency to *react* to life from a place of *low-frequency resistance* towards *Reality*.

**victim vocabulary:** distinct words or catch-phrases that perpetuate *victim consciousness* by blaming (or crediting) something outside ourselves as being the cause of our state of well-being. *Victim vocabulary* is a style of communication that evades self-responsibility and furthers the belief that we (and others) are at the mercy of life.

**witness, witnesses, witnessing, witnessing self, witnessing consciousness:** see *observer, observer consciousness*.

# *References*

Foundation For Inner Peace (1996). *A Course in Miracles*. New York, NY: Penguin Books, Ltd. (p. 573)

Frankl, V. (1959). *Man's Search For Meaning*. Boston, MA: Beacon Press.

Hambling, D. (February 2007). *Questioning Perceptual Blindness; I see no ships; European explorers found indigenous peoples unable to see their tallships - or did they?* www.forteantimes.com. www.forteantimes.com/strangedays/science/20/questioning_perceptual_blindness.html

Karpman, S. (1968). "The Drama Triangle". Fairy tales and script drama analysis. Transactional Analysis Bulletin, 7(26), 39-43. Retrieved from http://www.karpmandramatriangle.com/dt_article_only.html

Katie, B. & Mitchell, S. (2002). *Loving What Is*. New York, NY: Three Rivers Press. http://www.thework.com/index.php

Katie, B. & Katz, M. (2005). *I Need Your Love, Is That True?* New York, NY: Three Rivers Press. http://www.thework.com/index.php

Katie, B. & Mitchell, S. (2007). *A Thousand Names for Joy: Living in Harmony with the Way Things Are*. New York, NY: Three Rivers Press. www.thework.com/index.php

Katie, B. (2010). *Judge Your Neighbor Worksheet*. Retrieved June 10, 2010 from http://www.thework.com/downloads/worksheets/JudgeYourNeighbor_031810.pdf http://www.thework.com/index.php

Leloup, J. (2003). *Being Still, Reflections on an Ancient Mystical Tradition*. Mahwah, NJ: Paulist Press.

Supreme Science Qigong Foundation (SSQF). www.qigong.com

Small, J. (1990). *Becoming Naturally Therapeutic*. NewYork, NY: Bantam Books

Small, J. (1984). *Transformers: The Therapists of the Future*. NewYork, NY: Bantam Books

The Three Initiates (1912). *The Kybalion: A Study of the Hermetic Philosophy of Ancient Egypt and Greece*. Chicago, IL: The Yogi Publication Society Masonic Temple. *http://www.kybalion.org/*

Tolle, E. (1999). *The Power of Now: A Guide to Spiritual Enlightenment*. Canada: Namaste Publishing Inc.